NEW LEAVES

THE NEW
ADELPHI LIBRARY
VOLUME 23

The New Adelphi Library

Other titles in preparation

New Leaves

by
Filson Young

1 9 2 6

London: Martin Secker

Bibliography

First published 1915
Included in New Adelphi Library 1926

LONDON: MARTIN SECKER (LTD) 1926

Contents

On Opening a Letter

THERE are few habits of daily life which more clearly reveal character than one's method of receiving and opening letters. This is true whatever the time of day at which they arrive; but it can be most profitably observed at the delivery of the morning letters. They are the first event of the day, the first impinging of the outer world upon our personal lives, and as we have been without letters for twelve hours we have an appetite for them, as we have for breakfast. There are many ways of receiving one's morning letters; some people have them brought to the bedside, where they can be read and dealt with in privacy; such people come down to breakfast as though they had received no letters at all, and thereby deprive the curious among their fellows of a certain amount of entertainment. In other houses letters are laid out in little piles on a hall table; and this is an arrangement much more gratifying to the curiously minded, for if they come down early they can look at everyone else's pile of letters and at the same time remove their own from the vulgar gaze. A third method, characteristic of family life in modest establishments, is to have the letters disposed beside the plates on the breakfast-table; and this is the least satisfactory

7

to the retiring, and the most gratifying to the prying mind—except the intolerable but fortunately rare custom of having all the letters brought in to the head of the house, who examines them one by one, and distributes them to their rightful owners. There is a publicity in this arrangement which offends against all the ethics of private correspondence. There are many people who would not dream of opening or reading anyone else's letters, but who think nothing of commenting on the unopened envelope, saying, " I see you have a letter from So-and-so "—and then waiting to be told something of its contents. This habit, although it seems so harmless, may lead to the most fatal results ; it has in fact been the cause of more mortification, embarrassment, and downright deception than those who indulge in it ever realise.

There are all kinds of sensations and emotions precedent to the actual opening of letters. One becomes skilful in diagnosing their character and contents, and, even before the face of the envelope has been uncovered, the very edges of some of them will give rise to apprehension or hope. There are letters the mere sight of which gives one a troubled and anxious sensation ; everyone has his or her own particular brand. There are others which produce a sense of boredom ; we know so well all that the writers are likely to say, and that almost certainly there will be nothing of news or interest in them ; that it will be a weariness to read them, and that they will go immediately into the fire when read. There are a few—how few as life goes on !

8

—the sight of which gives one a thrill of delight ; and these, according to individual temperament, we either open greedily at first or reserve as a *bonne-bouche* for the last. It is when we are young that the receipt of letters in public—at the breakfast-table, for example—is most likely to cause us embarrassment, for in youth a business letter is a rare thing ; nearly all one's communications are of a personal character, and many of them are not unconnected with romantic emotions. We feel that the eyes of the breakfast-table—those deadly observant eyes of the surrounding family— are upon us ; if we do open the letter we shall have to read it under that fire of glances ; if we do not, we thereby advertise the fact that it is of too private and sacred a nature to be read in public. We feel it impossible, if we open it and read it, that some casual glance will not observe the disposition of writing on the front page—whether it begins with three short words like " My dear John " ; whether there are only two words (the longer one first), which can only be " darling " or " dearest " ; whether there is only one short word, which is certainly one of endearment ; or whether there is no line of apostrophe at all, and the front page is a solid block of writing—which conveys to the most careless straying glance the fact that a certain degree of intimacy has been reached between the writer and the reader. In the eyes of the embarrassed recipient the handwriting is magnified to several dimensions ; it seems impossible, as he turns to the second page, that the first cannot be read like a placard from half-way across the room. If by

9

any chance such a thing as a photograph or a flower falls out of the letter there is no possibility of concealing the fact ; and one sits there in agonised embarrassment, a leisurely study for the surrounding public of a Young Person Receiving an Affectionate Epistle.

But these things pass with the years, and as we grow older our correspondence become so diluted with the trivial and the commonplace that the most tremendous and fateful epistles can be received and opened without exciting any comment. But, having received your letters, how do you open them ? Do you turn them all over one by one from the top to the bottom of the pile and select one for opening ? Do you make a dash at the one that looks most interesting ? Do you begin at the top and go steadily through, reading and dealing with one letter before you open the next ? Do you methodically open all the envelopes first, and then take out their contents in turn and examine them ? Or do you choose here and there, taking either the most formidable or the most trivial first according as your nature is of the impulsive or cautious type ? Any of these methods will reveal a great deal about your character to the observant onlooker. Do you examine the envelope critically first, to see whether you know the writing ; or if that is un- familiar, look at the back to see if there is a crest or a cipher ; or, failing that, do you examine the postmark to see if that will give you any clue to the writer's identity ? Probably you do, because the one way of finding out whom a letter is from —opening and reading it—is only adopted by the majority of people after all other means have been tried. There is a childish pleasure in this brief moment of puzzledom akin in its small way to the abiding joy of opening a parcel containing a present, and wondering, as the successive wrappings are removed, what it is that they hide.

My average morning post contains the following items : A catalogue of second-hand books ; a green packet from the Press-cutting agency ; an invoice ; two statements of accounts rendered ; a confidential letter from a money-lender ; a notice in a halfpenny envelope of some kind of meeting ; an invitation or so ; a communication from some unknown reader ; a letter from a publisher, editor, or literary agent ; ditto from a lord mayor or duke telling me that as he has consented to take the chair at an annual dinner he thinks it a suitable occasion for me to subscribe largely to a charity ; and, only occasionally, a letter from some friend or relation on purely human and personal matters. There is not much room for variety in that, you would think ; and yet I go through the daily game of looking at them all in turn and hoping that there will be something so unfamiliar that I cannot diagnose it at once and will still be in doubt as to its contents when I open it.

But there are certain times when one receives letters which one fears to open, which one puts on one side unopened ; somehow, one thinks, the calamity or inconvenience which they herald will be put off as long as they remain unopened ; one's heart sinks at the sight of them, and one tries to pretend that they have not arrived. And there are certain frames of mind, in periods of depression or anxiety, when one will carry such a letter about with one for a day or two unopened. Sometimes when it is opened we find that it was not what we had feared, and that we have been suffering for nothing; but in any case, such a form of procedure is a sign that our equipment for the business of life is not what it should be; that we are below par, and ought instantly to take ourselves in hand, physically or mentally as the case may be, and get into a more courageous state of mind. The letter itself is nothing; if its news is ill, the ill has already happened and we cannot avert or prevent it; whatever it is, the sooner we know it and deal with it, the better for ourselves. Then there is the letter that tells you, quite suddenly and unexpectedly, that someone you cared for is dead. Such letters have a stealthy way of lying unimportantly among one's other correspondence; they get themselves taken up without scrutiny and opened mechanically while we are thinking of something else, and their dread message is suddenly spoken to us from the opened page. As one pauses with such a letter in one's hand and thinks back to the time when it was written or of which it tells, one sees with the mind's eye the letter hurrying on its way, in the post-cart, in the mail-bag, in the train flying over bridges and by river valleys and through sleeping towns in the darkness, to come and tell one that a part of one's life has been torn away and the world will never be quite the same again. How one remembers all the trivial things one has been doing during that time, unconscious that any blow had fallen; and how the tremendous fact made no difference at all by its actual happening, but only when the little letter came and told us that it had happened! And one thinks at such a time of how all the other letters are hurrying about the world by sea and land, being tied into bundles in the lighted post-office vans, or shot through pneumatic tubes, or jogging along on dark and scented country roads, dealing similar little blows at other little people all over the round world; and how the round world swings on into darkness and light, no slower for the joy, and no faster for the grief, that is thrilling on its surface!

There is one kind of caution with regard to letters, not cowardly, but merely a piece of legitimate prudence, which I strongly advise; and that is, never to read a letter the last thing at night. It requires a little determination; the pile of letters that comes by the late post and is left in your room shortly before you go to bed sometimes looks very harmless and alluring; but it is a good rule to have nothing to do with them. Not once in a hundred times can you take any action at that hour of the night which cannot as well be taken in the morning; and there may be matter in some of those letters which will disturb your tranquillity and set going trains of thought, tiresomely or even pleasantly exciting, by which your night's rest will not be improved. It is much better to make sure of sleep, and with it of the necessary degree of courage to open all your letters, whatever they may contain, in the morning.

On Getting Up Early

THERE are many things in life which ought to be governed by principle, but which in fact are governed by accident ; and among them our method of dividing the sleeping and working hours takes no unimportant place. Most people are agreed about the value of the early hours of the day, when there is no sense of hurry, and time seems to extend indefinitely before us. But the simple fact remains that few of us get up as early in the morning as we should like to. Our principle is that it is well to start the day in good time ; but the principle does not govern our actions. Accident, in the form of unpunctual housemaids, of occupations the night before, of disturbed sleep, and a hundred other things, steps in and prevents us from doing what we really wish to do. If I want to get up early in London, for example—as I sometimes wish to do in spring and summer—I am discouraged and deterred on every hand. My letters and newspapers, with which I begin the day, have not come ; but they will come while I am out, and lie unattended to until my return, and so make me actually later instead of earlier in beginning my morning's work. Then my clothes will not have been brushed, nor any hot water brought, nor any matutinal refreshment prepared; I shall move like an intruder in my own disordered rooms, and be a witness of scenes which are not intended for my eye. I know that the unsympathetic person will say that if I really want to get up I can wear another suit, wash in cold water, go without tea and toast, and keep out of the housemaid's way. Of course I can, and sometimes do. But all these things take away from the pleasure of getting up early; they make it appear as an eccentric and troublesome thing; it becomes actually inconvenient. You cannot lightly break in on the routine of domestic life in London. Your servants' arrangements are all made on the assumption that you will get up, say, at nine; and they silently resent, stubbornly obstruct, and finally defeat any attempt on your part to get up at seven. A whole world is against you, and you give it up, retaining only your principle and the fond belief that it is a good thing to get up early.

But in the country, where life is, or ought to be, much simpler in its habitual circumstances, how different! For the last four mornings I have been getting up two hours before my usual time; and am, in consequence, not free from that absurd pride in the fact which makes one wish to tell everyone about it, like a hen that has laid an egg. This, by the way, is one of the disagreeable associations of early rising. It has been treated too much as a virtue, and not enough as a luxury. People who get up early in the morning, instead of being looked upon as more fortunate and more luxurious than others, are held up as examples of virtue and

self-denial ; and their habits are enshrined in copy-
books, to the mortification of little children.
Children naturally like to get up early, and would
continue to do so if it were not for this copy-book
morality. When a thing is held up to them, not
as being pleasant and agreeable, but as something
uncomfortable which they *ought* to do, naturally
they will cease to wish to do it ; will soon actively
wish not to do it. And those of us who are ordinarily
human dislike the person who gets up earlier than
we, and who prates of it as if it were a virtue.
It is not a virtue ; it is only an advantage. Even
the copy-book philosopher recognises that : " The
early bird gets " . . . what ? A quiet heart, a
charitable soul, an increase of courage, or humanity,
or kindness ? Not at all. " The early bird gets
. . . the fattest worm ! " This clearly is not the
kind of virtue which is content to be its own reward ;
it demands to be paid for handsomely, and at
the expense of everyone else. The early bird
is well paid indeed ; for such payment every
company promoter, every City shark and sharper
would rise with the lark. Perhaps they do ; for
there is another ugly saying connected with early
rising : " You would have to get up very early
in the morning to get the better of So-and-so."
So this is the company of early risers, and this is
the spirit in which they practise their virtue !
Nice doings indeed on the moral upland lawn
where they go to meet the sun, and get the better
of each other ! Fortunately there are people who
are content with something less than the very
fattest prizes of life, and who can wait to take

quietly, and at their own time, what the greedy haste of the pushers has left for them.

So much for the absurd moral point of view about early rising. To me it is a piece of pure luxury and self-indulgence—far more so than sitting up late at night. As I have said, I think it is a mistake in town, where the world is not ready for its inhabitants before a certain hour. But tell me whether, for indulging in such pleasures as these, I should be praised for my great virtue, or envied for my good fortune. I opened my eyes at half-past six, and saw that the sun was shining. There were no preliminaries to be gone through ; no darkened rooms, untidy with the cigar-ends and empty glasses of midnight, to be traversed ; I had but to put on a pair of slippers, open a door, and step out through a smell of wallflowers on to the dewy grass. The sun, although low, was hot upon my back, and struck through the flimsy clothing to my delighted skin. The place was very remote, and there was no sound in the world at all except the choiring of birds. The trees in the garden were full of thrushes and finches ; the sky was alive with larks ; the larger trees outside the garden had their various loud-voiced inhabitants ; and from beyond this area, where notes could be distinguished, all round the inverted blue cup of the sky to the horizon a murmuring harmony, the invisible content of that cup, hummed and bubbled. There is a well of wonderful water in this garden ; and, having pumped until it began to flow ice-cold from the depths, I filled my glass, which instantly became covered with a frosty bloom, and sipped. A cloud-

less April morning in an English garden; the first
hot sunshine of spring; the smell of wallflowers;
the loveliest music in chorus from a thousand little
throbbing throats; and the taste and sparkle of
the coldest and purest of waters—I ask again, Is
the seeking of these things to be regarded as a virtue,
or as a piece of voluptuous self-indulgence?

But I do not ask for information: I know.

Under the Stars

SINCE first I discovered the joys of sleeping in the open air I have often made my bed under the stars when and where I could— on the high veldt of South Africa, on the decks of ships, on garden-lawns, on the summit of the Bass Rock, on the high cliffs of Cornwall, and by the seashore. There is not one of these resting-places that I cannot remember quite clearly as an occasion by itself, although that which I recall with the greatest pleasure is my sleeping-place on the turf at the very edge of the Bass Rock during a week of wonderful May nights, when I had the whole island to myself but for the gannets that wheeled and cried below me, the puffins, the seagulls, the rock-pipits, the rabbits, and a stray blackbird that used to come from the wood behind Tantallon Castle and whistle to me in the early morning. The least satisfactory of such alfresco slumbers have been those in a garden. In theory it is delightful to sleep on a lawn amid the radiant inhabitants and night perfumes of a garden ; but in fact there is something incongruous in the idea as well as in the practice of using a garden as a sleeping-place. Our occupation of it is so much associated with the sunshine and things of day that one feels like an intruder among plants and shrubs when they have gone to sleep at night ; and also, apart from its vegetable population, there are too many inhabitants of a garden, both winged and creeping things, to make it an entirely satisfactory sleeping-place. It seems delightful to be wakened by the song of birds ; but birds do not sing their best or their sweetest in the early morning. They are busy getting food and quarrelling over it ; and the sounds made by a colony of thrushes industriously tapping snails against stones and chirping loudly to one another concerning the preparation of breakfast are, however pleasant they may be when heard faintly through the closed curtains of a bedroom, altogether too noisy close at hand to make sleep easy or indeed possible. And as these sounds are in full blast at half-past four on a summer's morning one's hours of sleep are apt to be unduly curtailed by them.

But I remember one experience of sleeping out which proved also to be one of the simplest and best. I was staying in a cottage built literally on the beach of an unfrequented strip of the coast—a steep beach of shingle or gravel which each receding tide from spring to neap left piled in a series of little terraces that stretched down from the mark of the last spring tide to that of yesterday's high water. On the lowest of these, within six feet of the sea, my bed was spread ; a proximity that was made possible by the steepness and nature of the beach —and of course by the calmness of the weather ; for the sea here washed against the steep bank of shingle as against a wall and sent no intruding tongues of foam or showers of spray, like those which even a gentle surf spreads over a flat sandy shore. One might think that the stones of the shingle beach would make a harsh resting-place, even through a mattress ; but it was not so. The sea had smoothed the terrace quite level, and had carefully rounded and polished every individual stone so that it might give a little when thrust by its neighbour or by some superimposed weight ; and the flatness and support of a bed which thus rests on the actual surface of the earth give a comfort and repose of their own. This indeed I found one of the great advantages of the beach bed. Dryness and warmth are essential to one's comfort in sleeping out, and there are few spots of actual earth except, perhaps, in very dry weather, the heather of a mountain-side, which are so free from damp and exhalations of any kind as the bank of shingle close to the sea. In most other situations some kind of a camp bedstead is almost a necessity, and the fact that one is resting even a few inches from the earth makes a difference, and deprives one of that sensation of closeness to and unity with the actual stuff of the revolving world which one derives from lying prone on the ground. I lay flat on my back with my feet to the sea and the sunrise, as the dead lie, and found it a very comfortable and reposeful attitude. By turning my head a little the limits of my view were disclosed on either hand. To the north the horizon was the actual hog's back of the beach itself, a mile or so away ; to the right, and much nearer, it was bounded by a cliff that rose up like a wall cutting off the rest of the world.

When one is accustomed to it there is a sense of excitement induced by being thus out alone in the night which, after a period of indoor habit, keeps one awake and attentive long. One sleeps lightly too ; and though one awakes refreshed in the morning there has not been an hour in which one has not been aware of what was going on— the solemn changes of the stars, the shifting aspect of the sky, the gathering and grouping of clouds, and, above all, the voice of the sea which, speaking thus close to one's ear, is not monotonous, but full of an almost articulate though incomprehensible variety. One listens to it raking gently at the gravel, lifting and lapsing upon it, dragging it back a little and heaving its liquid breath again ; and thus listening one falls asleep, to be wakened half an hour later by some momentary change in its voice, some reinforcement of its energy thrilling to it here from the far-away Channel tides, or the last impulse of some unbroken wave that has rolled out from its unquiet heart, flowing across leagues of silence, to find voice at last against the shingle. And in such momentary intervals of consciousness one is aware of a change in the disposition of the stars, of the wheeling of the heavens above and spinning of the earth beneath one's head, and of the banking and massing of the clouds and changing colour of the steel-grey sky that tell of the coming of day. There were no inhabitants of this beach but two fishermen, who worked in a dreamy and deliberate manner with lobster-pots. They had a tiny shelter on the beach, in which by day they sat for hours scanning the horizon, or from which they at times issued and launched their boats, rowed out to where their creels were set, and so in again; moving slowly and stiffly up the beach like penguins, and settling again on their perch to scan the blank horizon. Very early in the morning, a good while before sunrise, which is about four o'clock at this time, I turned in my sleep and saw one of these men sitting on his customary perch, motionless, looking out over the sheet of rippled steel that the sea was at that hour. And I observed him there for at least ten minutes, fascinated by his immobility, almost guilty with the thought that I also was awake and intruding on his solitude; and, falling asleep, awoke again an hour later, when the sun was eating like a red-hot coal into the cloud-bank of the horizon, to see him sitting there still and gazing upon it.

I will not deny that on one morning it began to rain soon after sunrise. I was awakened by a pattering noise about my head and realised that the sky was heavy and dark, and that the rain which was beginning was no passing shower. With a curious cowardice I buried my head beneath the clothes, drew them over my pillow, and tried to go to sleep and forget about it; hoping that while I slept the clouds would disperse, and the sun shine out and dry my coverlet. But it was not so. The rain increased, pattering louder on the sheet, and presently a cold rivulet ran down beside my neck and warned me that, since I must sooner or later face the wet journey over the shingle to the house, I had better do it before I and my bed were soaked. There was something humiliating in being thus chastised by the elements whose intimacy I had sought, and something (I have no doubt) humorous enough to an onlooker in the sight of a wet draggled bed on the beach and a wet and thinly clad figure hurrying up to the house in the cold rain of dawn. But there was no onlooker; that made all the difference to my self-respect. The bed was dried again in the sunshine of the morning, and my appreciation of a dry bed in a bedroom, although it took nothing from the pleasure of the earlier part of the night, was by no means impaired by the fact that I had failed to carry out all my programme.

It would have been easy to contrive a tentlet over my pillow and waterproof cover over the bed, which would have made me independent of these gentle vicissitudes of a summer night; I have made such provision in other places where my situation was more permanent, and have found a quite separate and real pleasure in being thus snugly protected against rain and wind while lying out in the midst of them, and in observing, warm and dry, the passing over me of a storm of wind and rain. It is not really the weather that makes sleeping out difficult; that can easily be provided against. What is really essential and difficult to be sure of in England is privacy. I know not why, but the ordinary person has a singular shame in being observed by the public in his bed; and that shame is increased when the situation and method of his repose are anything out of the ordinary. Had this beach been a frequented beach, open to the passage of idle strangers, I confess that I should not have slept there. The pleasure which I had was a secret

and intimate pleasure ; I should have been shy
of strangers observing me enjoy it ; while the
possible facetious comments of the unromantic
prowler would have been quite unbearable. I
suppose there is something instinctive in this
unwillingness to be overlooked in our slumbers,
when we are off our guard and the masks we assume
in our waking hours are put away. But it is a
pity ; it makes what is a simple and pure pleasure
difficult and complicated to achieve. Indeed if we
do not mind lying open to the tremendous inquest
of the skies and the scrutiny of the sea and stars, we
need hardly fear the eye of our fellow-men ; for
the stars are never facetious, and the sea has no
curiosity.

Middle-Age Spread

THERE are tragedies that can be sung and acted; there are tragedies that can be spoken and read; and there are others that cannot be uttered, but are silently performed with shut doors in the mirrored secrecy of the soul. Here the solitary actor is also the spectator; it is the essence of the tragedy; for were an audience to be admitted the tragedy would in nine cases out of ten cease to be a tragedy and become a comedy or a farce. The solitary actor does not know this; and he goes on wringing his own heart with his performance, and (if the truth be told) nourishing a false sense of dramatic values. For pain and grief are solitary possessions; in so far as they are not or cannot be shared they sting and hurt, and in so far as they are shared they become inevitably dispersed and diluted, or perchance transformed and ennobled.

Among these secret tragedies few are more poignant than those connected with what is too often regarded as the doleful business of growing old. If growing old be really a tragedy, then is the whole of life a tragedy; the bursting of a seed-pod and the breaking of a blossom are tragedies, and the whole affair of existence an unmitigated evil. But this is not true ; and since the whole of life consists in growing old, since it is a process that begins from the cradle or the March seedfield, it is clearly something which is to be regarded as an essential part of life itself. I feel sure that on the whole the tragic view of life is the wrong one—if only because it makes life unbearable, and for an immense majority of people life is not only bearable, but extremely interesting and worth while. Although, however, we may be convinced that this is an obvious truth, it does not reconcile us to the process of growing old ourselves. We may see it as a beautiful development in other people, as a mellowing and ripening process ; but we are not a little shocked when we begin to realise quite clearly that it is also happening to us. The thought that we can never be young again is a sad thought ; but it is nothing to the realisation of the first moment when other people, whom we look upon as belonging more or less to our own generation, give clear evidence that they regard us in quite another light, and treat us either with the respect or the neglect that youth habitually accords to those who have passed the meridian of life. Again, the ageing of a beautiful woman is always something of a tragedy to herself ; and yet it is so obvious, it excites so much sympathy, that it can hardly be regarded as a secret tragedy, and so loses something of its bitterness. The real tragedy exists in the case of some plain man, the loss of whose youth can make little difference to his friends, since it carries no very obvious disabilities with it, when he first realises that in face and in figure he no longer looks like a young man.

For there is at first something quite absurd and incredible in the idea that this business of growing old can touch oneself. Most of us think of ourselves as being younger than we really are. There is, for example, such a thing as being thirty-seven. In a general way I should describe a man of thirty-seven as being in the full maturity of life, properly interested in grave matters, a vehicle of affairs, and bearer of responsibilities. Technically and by the calendar you are, say, thirty-seven ; but you cannot help feeling that the figures are extremely misleading in your case. You feel very much as you did when you were twenty-seven ; and then you felt the same as you did at twenty-four. You are not entirely preoccupied with the graver sides of life ; you often secretly long to share the amusements of children ; your shoulders seem unsuitable for heavy responsibilities ; it would be better to wait until you are more like what other people are when they are thirty-seven. You have still the 'sense that there is a long time yet in which to do the greatest and most serious things that you wish to do. Forty, you think, would be a good time to begin. Once you are forty there will be no getting away from the fact, and you will be willing to rank yourself with the middle-aged. But it is not true— when forty you will feel very much the same, and look upon fifty as a suitable age at which to take a more sober view of life. Imagine, then, with what a shock it must come to me to find that I am obviously regarded by many people as a sober, middle-aged person, one who will obviously prefer to sit with the elders, and who would be bored and mystified by the high-spirited doings of young people. With my contemporaries I feel I am acting a part—that I am only pretending, and pretending badly, to be a person with experience behind him ; I am always afraid of being found out. And yet when I am with my contemporaries of twenty-six it is only I who am quite at ease, and I perceive a tendency on their part to talk to me in a way that they think will interest me, deferring the more natural expression of themselves until I have left the room. I feel too young for the contemporaries of my age, and too old for the contemporaries of my spirit.

.   .   .   .   .   .

One day my tailor informed me that the measurements round my hips and my chest (I am glad it was not only the hips) had increased one inch since last they were taken. The dog actually laughed, and thought that the news would interest and amuse me. When he saw that I clearly regarded it as a disaster, he hastened to reassure me, saying, with a geniality for which I could have whipped him, " Why, sir, that's nothing at all ; it's only middle-age spread." Middle age ! How dared he use such an expression to me ? It rankled in my mind like a clumsy and ignorant affront, until, on soberly considering the matter, I realised that I had not only reached but had actually passed middle age, and that in the probable anticipation of life the years that remained to me must be less than the years that were gone. I know that this is a fact; I have earnestly tried to realise it, and have quite genuinely failed to do so. It means nothing to me. My brain receives the fact and automatically checks the logic of it, but I do not receive it with my whole intelligence. There must be a mistake; I must be an exception; and though it is on record that I was born in the year 1876 it is quite clear that my years have been shorter than other people's, that there must have been some group of years which went by at lightning speed, which became fused in the heat of passage and melted into one, and that the next decade will proceed at a much more reasonable pace.

There is no tragedy here, you see, because (for I think my experience is not an exception) we do not readily apply the fact of age to ourselves. But the Middle-Age Spread is another matter. There is no getting away from the tailor and his tape. There is the fact; and to go back to the tragedy of the plain man who was never valued for his beauty, and whom a touch of obesity cannot really depreciate, there is the real inner tragedy the moment when he looks in the glass and realises that his figure and his countenance are assuming a more fleshly habit. It may be desirable that we should see ourselves as others see us; but we wish also that other people could sometimes have the advantage of seeing us as we see ourselves. We look upon our image in the glass as no other eye looks upon us. No one may have noticed the youth and facial proportions of the plain man of my instance, but he noticed them; his face was interesting to himself, if to no one else; and the appearance of curves where once had been straight lines, and the rounding of what were once clean angles, is tragic to him; it is a tragedy which he can share with no one else. It is dreadful to him to see flesh where once he saw spirit, and to realise that he is well on the way to old age. For although, as I said, growing old is a constant process which begins at the moment of birth, it is one of which we are not continuously aware. There are times in youth when growing is painful and troubling, and a time in age when it is melancholy and solemn-ising. But there are long stretches in between when we are not very conscious of it, and for most men at any rate the years between twenty and forty bring with them little sense of growing old. Time is a stream that is always flowing, but where it is broad and deep we hardly notice the current; and we entertain ourselves on its shore, watching others floating by on the tide, until the moment comes when the current gets us too, and we realise that it is bearing us away. And for many people this moment is the moment when they first become aware of Middle-Age Spread.

It is a pregnant moment—almost, I think, the last great deciding moment in one's life. One must decide either to fight it or acquiesce. It is now, if ever, that we need to make a call upon our remaining youth, to summon it to our assistance. We may or may not decide to fight the spread of the body; we may or may not run to dietists and doctors and indulge in violent exercises. Whether that is worth while or not is largely a matter of individual circumstance ; but what we must see to is that the spread of the body does not communicate itself to the mind, and result in a fatuous acquiescence in our destinies. This is the moment at which people first drift out of sympathy with what is young and bold in life and in thought. They think it merely silly ; they see all its fallacies, without sufficiently respecting its vitality and renovating influence. The mind which has been attacked by Middle-Age Spread expresses a quite angry contempt for young and daring ideas, more especially—and this is strangest of all—if it was once daring and rebellious itself. "Why," says middle age, "I have been through all that ; I once thought like that, there is nothing in it," and if it were really honest it would add, "The only things there can really be anything in are the things which were new when I was young. They were real and inspiring things ; they have come to something ; I represent them ; but these are shams, the silly ideas of very young people who have not had the advantage of being born when I was born."

One has only to state this position to see the pathetic futility, the entire negativeness of it ; and yet how many of us who have reached middle age can boast that we have never felt, if we have not uttered, a like sentiment ? So I would say to all who are beginning mentally or physically to spread : Have patience with the new generation ; be interested in and curious about them ; do not laugh their futurism and cubism entirely out of court ; if it is nothing itself it means something ; there is something behind it ; there is your own lost youth behind it. Have patience with them, encourage them, and, above all, do not lose touch with them; lest haply even the current which bears you along discards you and leaves you floating in some backwater, spreading, and spreading, and spreading.

On Calling in the Doctor

ONE of the most sobering events of middle age is the first realisation that one's health is a thing that must be taken care of, and that one's body will resist undue demands upon it. Hitherto we have been busy with other things, and in the glorious crowded morning-time of life have had little time or necessity for preoccupations as to the maintenance of physical health. We took it as a right and a matter of course, like the air we breath and the water we drink. But afterwards, in that trying time when a man must realise that his youth is gone, that the season of hope and promise is over, and that from now to the end it must be either performance or remembrance, it comes upon him with sometimes painful realisation that attached to, mysteriously involved with, his eager and still aspiring spirit, is a creature of flesh, which shows signs of rebellion, and even—oh horror !—of decay. With something like shame and humiliation he realises that this physical machinery is of immense importance in hindering or furthering his prime activities. Memories of that happy period when the flesh was no burden assail him ; he becomes increasingly conscious that he has a vile body, and wistfully dreams of a glorious body.

On Calling in the Doctor

It is then that, with something like desperation, we begin to cast about us in the search for some remedy for disease, or some conserving elixir of life. Youth and health themselves have little preoccupation with such matters; it is middle age and the age that follows it, and broken health and the symptoms of disease which set man forth on the quest of the glorious body, or of someone who will help him to attain it.

I may say at once that I have never yet found the ideal doctor. My indispositions are few and simple, and of a kind for which conscience rather than science indicates the treatment; so my opportunities of choice have been few. And one's choice is rather more limited than appears. I live in a part of London which is much inhabited by doctors; their plates gleam upon every hand as I walk to my own door. I feel that I would like to try them all, but an inherent sense of loyalty keeps me faithful to one, expecially as when he was first called in he had the tact carefully to inquire into my habits, and to explain that none of the things I enjoyed most was bad for me, provided, etc. But sometimes unworthy doubts assail me. I wonder whether, by employing some other doctor, I might not enjoy buoyant health without any moderation at all. And then I look at the brass plates as a child with a shilling to spend looks in at various shop windows, and wonder, supposing I were to make a change, in which quarter my money would be best expended. The mere brass plate or condition of the hall door no longer deceives me. I have seen the shabbiness behind too many smart

35

hall doors to take them as an indication of anything at all except a desire to keep up appearances. Window curtains and the condition of the windows themselves are a much better guide ; but all these externals are really fallacious ; and there is no safe guide to the choice of a doctor except by actual trial. Even that is apt to be disappointing, as in the case of Carlyle, who thus describes the attempt to deal with one of his hygienic crises :

" I had ridden to Edinburgh, there to consult a doctor, having at least reduced my complexities to a single question : Is this disease curable by medicine, or is it chronic, incurable except by regimen, if even so ? This question I earnestly put ; got response, ' It is all tobacco, Sir ; give up tobacco.' Gave it instantly and strictly up. Found after long months that I might as well have ridden sixty miles in the opposite direction, and poured my sorrows into the long hairy ear of the first jackass I came upon, as into this select medical man's, whose name I will not mention."

And even when we do try a new doctor, how many of us want the same thing from him ? If we are really ill of course we want to be made well ; but the majority of a doctor's work is attendance on people who are not really very ill at all and to whom his visits are a luxury. I confess that I like extremely to be visited by the doctor. I cherish the thought that a man who has spent years in the arduous and difficult pursuit of exact scientific knowledge is concentrating the whole of his resourceful experience upon me. I feel sure that he cannot fail to be struck by the peculiarity and

exceptional interest of my case ; and here I may
point out that the first duty of a desirable doctor
is to appear to be so struck and impressed. If he
does not, the awful thought seizes me that famili-
arity with disease has made him contemptuous of
it and that his perceptions are dulled by custom.
He may be blind to the vital significance of my
symptoms. Nothing therefore that he can do can
restore him to my confidence. If I get worse it
is through his blunder ; if I get well it is owing
to the inherent nobility of my constitution. And
in either case I inevitably regard him as a man who
may be very well for ordinary, everyday people, ·
but who is unworthy to attend upon me.

Then there is the doctor who takes you too
seriously, and he is the most undesirable of all.
He forbids you this and that, and tells you that
you must not smoke at all for three weeks, and
also gives you other commands which, as he ought
to know, any child would disobey. You do not
choose him a second time. Perhaps the most
alluring type of doctor is he who flatters you by
assuming that you have a scientific knowledge
almost equal to his own, and who discusses your
symptoms, not in insulting language which you
can understand, but in terms which he would
employ if he were consulting with a fellow prac-
titioner. He takes you into his confidence as it
were. He says, "I am not going to give you
medicine because you are quite sensible enough
not to believe in it. I have found that a little
dry champagne in these cases works wonders ;
but there is one thing you must on no account

touch, and that is sherry." Here he draws a bow, pretty safely, at a venture, hoping that you detest sherry. If, on the other hand, it should have proved to be a really bad shot, and that you really are fond of sherry, he will say, " Very well, then, a glass or two of dry sherry ; but, remember, no champagne ! " The two tastes hardly ever go together. The ideal doctor will proceed on a system of this kind, but he will, in addition, cure you. That is essential. What one asks from a doctor is, in short, that he will employ the particular kind of manner and method which is most attractive to you, and that he will, in addition, get rid of your ailment. It is asking a good deal, I admit, but one does ask a good deal from doctors ; and, to do them justice, one sometimes gets it.

There is no doubt that the old type of family physician had this great advantage over men of the more modern school—that he did acquire the knack of approaching every case with a gravity and seriousness, or appearance of gravity and seriousness, which were very reassuring to the patient. Something of the mystic, or at any rate some sense that there is a mystery in the healer's art, was part of the equipment of the old physician. The modern attempt to treat the practice of medicine as an exact science has not been entirely successful. The truth is that healing is an art, and not a science. It is an art of which science is the handmaid, not a science with a little art thrown in. And when this is understood, all the gravity, all the mystery, and all the ritual that accompanied the old " bedside manner " have a certain use and propriety. How wonderful is the sensation of confidence and hope which a really impressive manner, backed by a sound knowledge and experience, can inspire in a sick person ! You may say that it is the knowledge and experience that effect the cure, and not the manner ; and yet we have all known cases in which the most undeniable attainments, being allied with an awkward, diffident, or unsympathetic manner, have failed to inspire just that degree of confidence that will induce a patient to make the little effort that may be vital to recovery. We all have our superstitions ; in the slums it is the exhibition of some black and nauseous draught which inspires the patient with confidence in his doctor's ability ; in my case the draught must be of a little more subtle and delicate kind, and be administered *per aurem* instead of by the mouth ; but the difference is only the difference of composition ; the draught or the cachet, the bolus or the linctus, must still be administered. Our beneficent Government now makes the doctors a certain allowance for the drugs they use ; but I fear they will make them no allowance for, and so probably discourage, the use of those more subtle, intellectual applications which give such variety and such pleasure to the experience of being mildly out of sorts.

Thirst

IT is one of the few privileges of the dyspeptic
that he thoroughly understands what thirst
is, and consequently thoroughly enjoys the
quenching of it. Not for him the moderation
of the exasperatingly well-balanced man who, in
the hottest weather, only moistens his lips with a
little water, or at the most washes out his mouth
but does not swallow the cooling liquid. No; the
dyspeptic requires his drinks to be very long, and
either very cold or very hot, and when in hot
weather the dyspeptic hears the tinkle of ice and
glass, and sees the dullness of frost on the outside
of the tumbler, he knows that one of the pleasantest
physical sensations procurable for him in this world
is at hand. His imagination is stirred, not only
by the thought of liquid matter passing down his
throat, but by the artificial differences of temperature which he is about to produce; by the idea of a
cold glacial stream being poured into the arid desert
of his system.

In all imaginative people—and in this matter the
imagination of the dyspeptic is hypersensitive—
the sensation of thirst is almost as much a literary
sense as it is a physical one; it is extraordinarily
stimulated by words and ideas. Most of us know
some particular food or drink, the desire for which

is stimulated in us by reading about it. But the writing must be skilful, or, if not skilful, artlessly good. The cruder method of the stage produces the same effect; all smokers have experienced the almost overwhelming desire to smoke which comes upon them when some one lights a cigarette on the stage; and on me, at any rate, those strange and rapid restaurant meals of the fashionable theatre, when a party sits down at a table and is whirled through six courses in about five minutes, surrounded by champagne bottles in ice buckets and trays of liqueurs, have an absurdly exciting effect. It is an entirely imaginary hunger which I suffer on these occasions, for if I were to be suddenly led forth and given a seat at the feast, I probably could not eat anything; but sitting helplessly in my stall, half an hour after dinner, I suffer all the pangs of starvation. And the literary stimulation of these symptons is exactly the same thing on a somewhat higher scale. Tobacco, food, and drink are the things which most lend themselves to this kind of treatment—one may call it verbal hypnosis. It is a science as yet only partially understood by advertisers; when it is fully understood advertisements will only be written by the most skilful and imaginative literary artists.

The treatment of food and drink in literature, and especially of drink and thirst, is one of the most interesting of the minor literary studies. Some of the greatest authors, and some who have treated the subject most freely, have never understood it. Dickens, for example, who was a master in the literary treatment of the more homely kinds of

food, never really understood drink. *Pickwick* is
full from cover to cover of brandy and water, hot
and cold, but chiefly cold—a most nauseous drink,
and, what is more to the purpose, not one of the
drinks which lend themselves to true literary
treatment. It is only the very simplest drinks that
are suitable, because it is not appetite or the palate
which can be appealed to by verbal hypnotics
so much as the elementary sensation of thirst.
Water is easily, therefore, the chief fluid for which
desire can be created by the literary method. The
Bible contains all the classical examples of the
literary treatment of water, whether in the form of
seas, or rivers, or streams, or fountains, or mere
reviving draughts. And, next to water, which
really stands by itself, as one of the elements, the
best drinks for literary purposes are milk, tea and
coffee. The point is not so much whether you like
these drinks above all others, as whether, if you
read about them in skilful writing, you may be
brought to imagine that you greatly like and desire
them. Personally I think milk is a delicious drink,
although many people do not like it ; but I could
guarantee to make it appear delicious to anyone in
half a page of writing. The last word on tea was
not Cowper's much-quoted and rather artificial
" cup that cheers but not inebriates " ; but Lamb's
simple phrase " whole goblets of tea," which, in a
quite incredible way, can produce in the ordinary
reader in an arm-chair all the sensations of fatigue,
heat, and refreshment by tea. Coffee comes into a
rather different category ; for literary purposes it
should never be used but in connection with cold,

as a heating and reviving thing. The proper group of words is " hot coffee and rolls," which, even used with moderate skill and a little atmosphere of wintry weather, or exposure to a snowstorm on the top of a coach, will generally produce an overwhelming desire for coffee in the minds even of people who dislike it. But there, for English readers, the list almost ends. You can make a Frenchman thirsty by writing about wine, but not an Englishman ; and beer, when you have rung all the changes on " nut-brown " and " foaming tankards," is a strangely disappointing stuff for literary purposes. I like beer very much, but I have never been made thirsty for it by reading except in one case, where a character of Mr. Arnold Bennett's, who is drinking beer, keeps wiping his mouth with the back of his hand, and ejaculating at intervals one word, " Beer ! "—nothing else. This, I think, must be accepted as the correct treatment of beer in literature.

Thackeray stumbled heavily in the matter of drink in his books ; " potations of cold brandy and water " is a phrase which he frequently employs—a phrase both deplorable in itself and for the images it conjures up. Meredith wrote zestfully of Claret, of Port, of vintage champagne and the greater wines of Burgundy and the Rhine and even of Ale ; but he deals with nothing so simple as thirst, and he keeps you waiting for your drink while he spins long and highly artificial essays on the philosophy of bubbles. Mr. Thomas Hardy on the other hand, is faithful to cider, which in his hands, but in his hands only, becomes one of the classical literary drinks worthy to rank with the wine of Greece, the water of the Bible, and the tea of Charles Lamb. Such things as lemonade and ginger-beer are utterly useless for literary purposes ; the nearest thing that one could get to them would be lime-juice—but you must not call it lime-juice ; you must call it " the juice of a fresh lime squeeezed into a tumbler of cold spring water." As a matter of fact, lemon-squash is a far pleasanter drink than lime-juice ; but by the literary method I would undertake to make ten people want to drink lime-juice for one that I could make want to drink lemon-squash.

This literary stimulation of appetite is a very real thing. I remember that when I was a very little boy I used, in the interval between breakfast and going to church on Sunday mornings, to be given a book called *Line upon Line* to read, and I used regularly to go through the following remarkable ritual. I used to turn up the passage about Elijah being fed by the ravens ; the words in the narrative were, " And the ravens used to bring Elijah bread and meat." There was a woodcut of the prophet sitting in a kind of rocky grotto in a dressing-gown and very long beard, with the ravens giving him in their beaks slices of bread, apparently cut from a loaf, with slices of what looked like sirloin laid upon them. When I had read this passage and looked at the picture, I used to go down to the larder where certain foods were always prepared in advance on Sundays. Among them was a plate containing slices of a kind of currant-bread buttered ; one of these I used to abstract and eat, carefully arranging the others so that its absence should not be noticed. It represented to me the bread and meat of the picture. No other substance would have been of the least use to me ; there were many things I liked better in the larder, but it was for this that the sacred work had created an appetite, and this alone which would satisfy it. The time must have been about an hour after breakfast, so it cannot have been genuine appetite ; it was false, or literary, appetite.

But let me put my own theories to the test. Probably you do not like buttermilk, or more likely, you do not know what it really is. Fast disappearing now in the days of patent separators and agricultural co-operation, it was in my childish days an honoured drink in Ireland, and among the poor more than that—" food and raiment both," as I have heard an old peasant ejaculate after a deep draught of it, while indeed some surplus drops were adorning his coat. But the buttermilk of my memory is associated with the most wonderful larder, lying deep in the stone outworks of an ancient house, lit dimly at one end by a door veiled with boughs of jasmine, and giving on to a walled garden, and at the other end open-ing, by mysterious partitions, into a store-room sacred to the mistress of the house where one was given delicious things to eat, and whence there came always a faint odour of spices. Out of the glare of the strong sunshine and play among the salt spray and surges of the shore I would come as a child into this magic world of coolness and darkness. At the far end of the larder stood always a great crock or jar kept half full of buttermilk, with a dipper hanging on the side, and cups and glasses always there for the use of the thirsty children of the house. Out of the glare, I say, from one's toiling play by the loud seashore, one would hurry for a moment into this cool and fragrant darkness. The crock was very thick and of a coarse substance, allowing a certain amount of evaporation, so the buttermilk was always very, very cold. The dipper would be seized and the cold depths of the crock gently agitated ; up would come the dipper, dripping snow and milk and ice ; the cup would be filled, a deep breath fetched, and the nectar, cold, astringent, and aromatic, would be drained with great gulps and sighs. The dipper would be returned and sink with a gurgle into the buttermilk ; and children emerging from the larder would appear to be wearing a small white moustache. And as we came out thus from the cool darkness, the wind and the sun and the sea, rough playfellows of our childhood, would greet us like brothers.

Innocent, delicious draught ! More potent still than any drug to conjure visions of gardens and the sea, and to bring back the dream scents of salt and honey and jasmine and verbena ; but powerless as any cup of Circe, or any draught of Lethe, to quench that most divine of thirsts, the thirst of the soul for its own youth, and the good things that are gone.

Accessories

I HAD occasion the other day to turn out an old box which had lain for years in a lumber-room, in which someone had from time to time put away things which I had ceased to use. This was long enough ago for me to have forgotten completely what the box contained, and when I opened it, and began to discover its contents, it was like a journey back into time. I found, as it were, layers of my former self, some of them very early indeed ; and the material of these layers was chiefly composed of the accessory rubbish which accumulates round some hobby or interest. The first thing I came upon was a motoring layer —goggles, gloves, road-books, and the like. Then a war layer, dating from my war-correspondent days in South Africa—odds and ends of weapons, maps, spurs, filters, and articles of camp equipment. Then there was a photographic layer, consisting of a number of printing frames, chemicals, and elaborate devices for taking perfect photographs, and along with them, spotted and fading even in the darkness of the trunk, were some of the truly lamentable results of my effort. Lower down still were indications, dim and fragmentary, but conclusive, of a cycling period—clips, a tin of some patent fraud for imitating silver plating, a

47

device for expanding forks, and a map ; and at the
very bottom evidences of another and much
earlier and cheaper photographic period, where the
fragments were on a very small and inexpensive
scale, and less remotely connected with the actual
processes of crude photography. All these deposits
represent interests and occupations which have
waxed and waned. And, although there is nothing
which appears so absolutely worthless as the
accessories, extinct as an old love, of an abandoned
hobby, yet it is always wise to keep them, for one
never knows when oneself or someone else afterwards may come round to them again. At the
moment of this discovery I did not possess a motor-
car or a bicycle, and my interest in military equipment had ceased to be a personal one. On the
other hand, I had just started on a new period of
photography ; I was in the act of accumulating an
entirely new set of impedimenta, and was even
capable of taking an indulgent and patronising interest in the obsolete accessories of five years before.

There are men and women to whom the chief
interest of anything lies, not in its centre, but in its
circumference ; and who at heart really care more
for the accessories of some sport, or hobby, or
work, than for the thing itself. I confess to being
one of these people. There is evidently a huge
number of us, because vast departments of
commerce batten upon us, and on the foundation
of our voracious appetite has been built up the
modern science of newspaper advertising. We
seldom excel in any of our occupations ; that is
another matter altogether, reserved, as a rule, for

the man whose equipment of implements is of the very simplest, although of the best. But for me the mere duty of the thing is nothing; it is the extent to which the doing of it can be complicated and diluted by the employment of complementary machinery that has always appealed to my immoderate fancy. Thus, when at school I learnt carpentry, I was all agog for it until a complete set of tools had been purchased; then my interest rather evaporated. Failing actual accessories, printed matter will, to some extent, satisfy an appetite like this, and when I have bought a dog and equipped him with collar and lead, and found that there has been little more scope in this direction, I have fallen back on various works upon the management and breeding of dogs. When I had a horse I haunted the saddlers and the corn merchants, and ran riot in currycombs, body-brushes, blankets, headstalls, and hoof polish. In my early motoring days my car was more like a Christmas-tree than a car, so many things were fastened upon it; and as for photography, although I could never take a decent photograph, there was hardly a chemical, or a kind of dish, or a device for handling prints, or a pattern of mount that I had not tried. Within a fortnight of my beginning the game of golf I had read eight books on the subject and possessed about a score of clubs. So inveterate is my taste for accessories that I am even capable of that advanced form of the appetite which consists in an appreciation of the accessories of some occupation of which one is entirely ignorant; so that I have found myself in idle moments gazing with the eye of desire upon collections of copper utensils for the use of cooks, and on various powders, pastes, and implements connected with cleaning with which the windows of a certain kind of shop are filled.

The first necessity, both to the accessory-monger and to the victim of the habit, is a catalogue. Whether your hobby be the collection of postage-stamps or the keeping of ferrets, a catalogue is the first thing to have. There you find set forth the different kinds of mounts and albums to which the stamps can be set, the different kinds of hutches and food utensils which the ferrets can use. What gardener does not know the joys and temptations of the catalogue, with its glowing descriptions of trees and plants? What though, when they arrive, they appear as almost indistinguishable little bundles of mud? It is their printed description that matters. Brooms and brushes, too, are things which are very attractive accessories in any hobby, whether it be gardening or painting; and they come into a great many. There is no hobby so humble that it has not got its parasite host of accessory providers, each with his catalogue. You would hardly think, for example, that there would be much room for the indulgence of this passion in connection with goldfish; yet I can assure you from experience that the possession of a tank of fishes led in my case just as surely to the accumulation of accessories as the possession of a motor-car. Even the aquarium man had a catalogue—a mean document and ill-spelled, but enough to account for all my pocket-money for

the time being. I remember two entries in it to
this day : " Hot-water grown Valisneria, 2*d.* a
bunch ; monster bunch, 3*d.*" ; and " Water-beetle,
Dityscus, rows himself like a boat, 6*d.*" I suppose
the humblest of all hobbies is the keeping of
birds ; yet the man who keeps a few linnets is
catered for, not only in catalogues, but in a whole
mass of contemporary journalism called the Fancy
Press, in which his appetite is stimulated by the
announcement of a new line of " tin drinkers,
4*d.* a dozen " ; " cock larks, 8*d.*, 9*d.* ; fierce in song,
1*s.* ; giants, 1*s.* 3*d.* " ; or " Hartz Mountain
canaries, bold birds, guaranteed cocks, not half
hens, very fierce in song, daylight or gaslight "—to
say nothing of an endless variety of inexpensive
rubbish in the form of foods, medicines, perches,
nests, cages, and implements made of wire and
pottery.

Well, and why not ? We can only live once,
and the more we live the better ; and I find upon
examination that the passion for accessories is
only an expression of a passion for life. Not to
follow up those engaging byways of temptation is
to miss a great deal of agreeable and accidental
information and knowledge of the kind that
makes life full and interesting. You can press the
button of your camera and send your films to be
developed and remain unenlightened ; but if you
equip yourself with half its accessories, photography will lead you far into the sciences of physics
and chemistry. If you have a horse and someone
to look after him you need not occupy yourself
very much about his needs ; but if you have this

interest in accessories and take a pleasure in thinking, not how little, but how much, you can do towards making your horse's stable a kind of shrine, it will not only bring you nearer to him and make you understand him better, but it will make you understand a great many other things, such as the rotation of crops and the working of leather. In short, accessories are the circumference of the circle of which the thing itself is the centre ; they are leads and links which take us out from ourselves (and at our own expense) into the surrounding life of the world.

Fear

IN my sleep in the stillest part of the night I
became aware that something was moving.
One of those outlying sentries of the brain
which seemed to be empowered to deal with
minor disturbances without awaking the general
intelligence registered it at first simply as movement,
although not of a kind sufficient to alarm or awake
me. But it was persistent; and, like one view
dissolving into another on a screen, the state of
dreams gradually gave way to a state of consciousness.
Something was moving in the room, rustling and
fidgeting with a noise that suggested some soft
substance in contact with wires. I thought at first
that my goldfinch, who dreamed on a perch not far
from my bed, was stirring in his sleep; but I had
known him for years, and it was his habit to sleep as
soundly as his master, and to make no movement
until, when the curtains were withdrawn, he sang a
short *réveillé* and descended to his breakfast of teazle
and thistle and cornflower seeds. But the noise continued; it was something like the sound of a bird
jumping and fluttering in a cage; and, alarmed
lest some malady should have visited my old friend,
I slid out of bed and switched on the light. The
noice ceased absolutely. There was my goldfinch
with his crimson head under his brown wing, fast

asleep in his accustomed place, and nothing stirred in the room. Not a little puzzled, I went back to bed and tried to sleep; but I had not been unconscious for many minutes when I was again aroused by the rustling and leaping, this time accompanied by an actual chirping which made me think that Sir Japp Silk (for that was the goldfinch's name; he used to be called Mr. Silk, and was created a baronet after his last moult) must be indulging in a seizure of some kind. But a certain definiteness in the sound directed my attention to the top of a cupboard in another part of the room, and there I remembered that an empty birdcage had been placed. I lay and listened; certainly the sounds came from there, but they were the sounds of some creature demented, rustling and scrambling, shrieking and tumbling within the wires of the cage. And suddenly I remembered that some seed had been left in the bottom of the cage; some hungry mouse toiling up the stairs of three storeys had discovered it, and was rioting and rejoicing in the possession of so excellent and abundant a repast. I stole out of bed and again switched on the light, and as the room sprang into brightness the scrambling stopped, and a dark object with a tail leaped out of the cage, ran along a shelf and down a curtain, and disappeared behind a chest. I went back into bed, but had not been there five minutes before the scrambling recommenced, and with it the leapings and squeaks of excitement. I had left the light on and had only to open my eyes and look; and there sure enough was the mouse, nibbling and jumping with strange antics on the floor of the cage. I sat up; he turned and looked at me; and in the same instant fear laid hold upon him and me. We looked at one another in terror. Until he had seen me I had been conscious only of interest; but now that he was alarmed and stood for a paralysed moment before running away, I was conscious of being thoroughly frightened. I am not more fearful than most people, and in moments when danger of any kind has threatened me I have only been aware of a slightly increased interest in life; but now I was conscious of fear, and could actually hear my heart thumping within me. For a moment the mouse stood up and looked at me, and then, with an incredible darting furtiveness, disappeared.

I turned the light out and lay down again thoroughly shaken, my nerves on edge and my senses on the stretch for the first warning of the creature's return. I tried to quiet myself by analysing this preposterous emotion; but I could come to no other conclusion than that it was the fear in the mouse's heart which had evoked and awakened fear in mine; and I tried to comfort myself with the reflection that I was only exemplifying in my own person the truth that fear begets fear. But my peace had been wrecked; and uncanny terror had entered my quiet room and inhabited there with me. I could not spend another night like that; so on my instructions a trap was set, and by the time I retired to rest the next night I had forgotten my fear. But I was again awakened in the dead of night by scratching and chirping—this time, alas, from the place on the floor where the trap had been set. I tried to endure this for a little while, but fear and compassion both wrought in me to such an extent that I rose and gingerly picked up the trap, and, with a sinking heart, carried it to a place of execution. There by a familiar machinery I created a maelström, and, shutting my eyes, opened the trap and violently shook it. When I looked again the trap was empty and the mouse had disappeared. I returned to my couch literally shaking, and feeling like a murderer.

But, having embarked on this fatal path, I felt I must continue. Perhaps there were two mice; if so, justice must be done upon the second one; I would not have fear in the room with me. Again the trap was set, and again in the chill hours of the dawn I heard the scratchings and whimperings of a second prisoner. I lay and considered the horrors of the previous night, and that I must now rise and repeat them; and my blood froze at the thought. Not again, by my hand, that murderous act! I would leave it until the morning and let other hands do the fell deed. And I began to count the hours until my servant should call me and bring relief; but sleep had fled, the whimpering voice continued, and I could bear it no longer. Once more I rose up, determined to cast out fear once and for all. I grasped the trap, but as I approached the place of execution my heart totally failed me and my feet refused to continue in the way. Instead, I took another direction, turned downstairs still carrying the trap, until I had reached regions of the house quite unfamiliar to me. And here (to be truthful) I opened the trap and enlarged the mouse ; and the last I saw of him was a disappearing tail that fled through an open grating to freedom and the vicinity of stables.

With a light heart I returned, and, with a perfect inward confidence that it would not be needed, reset the trap and returned to bed, and slept sweetly and dreamlessly until the morning. When I awoke the trap still gaped ; and since that day neither mouse nor fear has visited me while I sleep.

The Teaching of Golf

I HAVE been studying the literature of golf, especially that part of it devoted to the instruction of beginners, and I am astonished to find how little the expert seems to know, or how much he seems to have forgotten. It is the beginners who should write the books; it is they who really know everything about the game, though they cannot play it. Their minds are stored with a magazine of theory and of method that contains all the advice of all the experts. That the expert has forgotten all about the game except how to play it is apparent from the kind of advice he invariably gives to the beginner. There are several types of book on golf. The type most familiar is the general book on the game, such as was written by most of the famous champions of my youth. The plan of such books is always the same. There is, first of all, a chapter on the history and origin of the game; and, as nobody knows its origin, this chapter generally consists of a more or less diffuse statement of that fact. The next chapter is probably called " The Choice of Clubs." The beginner is told that there are a great many kinds of clubs, that he must not get too many, and that he must not get too few. There are good clubs and bad clubs, he is told, and the advice of the expert is, all things considered, that he should get good ones, but he had better put himself into the hands of a professional and let him choose his clubs for him ; he will know better than the beginner.

It is from this moment that the repressive and discouraging attitude towards the beginner is apparent. That innocent soul, who has taken up the game with the idea of getting some pleasure from it, is told pretty roundly that he had better not attempt to do this for a long time. If he is doing anything pleasant with his clubs, such as hitting the ball with them, or happily carving his way round the links, he is told that he can never learn to play golf that way. If he light-heartedly wishes to go and choose a set of handsome clubs, he is ordered to throw them away, and go and put himself in the hands of a professional, and take what he is given. Perhaps the next chapter in the book is on balls, and the beginner learns that there are many kinds of balls, good and bad, the chief difference being that the good ones fly true and the bad ones do not. Here the advice as to clubs is reversed. The beginner must not buy good balls ; any old thing will do for him. When he is an expert, then he may put down on the tee a glossy " zone-zodiac " or a shining " colonel " ; in the meantime, any common, rough, uninteresting ball will do for him. It is almost suggested that it would be bad for him to play with a good ball. At any rate, let him put himself in the hands of a professional, who will sell the necessary balls to him. The next chapter, on learning to play the game, is, as a rule, equally dispiriting. The beginner must not try to play; he must not even use his new balls or his clubs, or go on the links at all. Let him stand in his own room and swing with an old umbrella for a month or two, when, if his spirit be sufficiently broken, he may be stood out in the corner of a meadow with an old club and a gashed ball to take his first lesson in using the sacred implements. That is the burden; he must not try to play or enjoy himself; he must practise. He is seriously advised to go into some " quiet corner " with a ball and a club to practise the same stroke over and over again, replacing the turf every time, then going and fetching his ball, hitting it again, replacing the turf, and so on —as if anyone could continue such an occupation for more than ten minutes without going out of his mind. The beginner is told that the swing is everything, and that the full swing is the supreme joy and perfection of golf. He is also told that he must not attempt to swing. Let that be reserved for the finished player; the beginner must be content with something else which is never quite clearly defined, but it must be something without joy or satisfaction in it. And there, suddenly, advice to the beginner ends. The next chapter is probably on the mashie, a club the pupil so far has not been allowed even to buy, with elaborate hints as to imparting under-spin and cut to the ball, and the different tactics to be employed if one wishes to play a stroke of a hundred yards or only of ninety-nine. Out swims the expert into the wide sea of talk and theory, leaving the unhappy beginner with a brassie (a club of which he is in dread), a cleek (which he fears and hates), and an iron, whose only apparent use to him so far has been as a turf-cutter.

There is another type of book written by someone who has adopted some patent grip or stance of his own and won an open championship. In order to impress his patent on the public he, too, must write a complete book on the game of golf, the frontispiece of which probably consists of a large photograph of his hands tied in a knot, or a ground-plan of his feet. This contrivance and its bearing on the game are discussed through some three hundred pages, and at the end he probably says: "Although this is the only correct method in golf, I do not advise it for the beginner; let him be content," etc. etc.

Then there is the other little book of a very disarming kind, and more dangerous than any. In it the writer seeks to brush aside all that has been written by anyone else. Let the beginner attend to these few simple pages, and it is promised that, if he does not become a champion, he will at least have no difficulty in acquiring a good steady game, and have a handicap of not more than six. The student sighs with relief, and thinks that here, at any rate, is something that he can master; and it is a very alluring method. The secret is that you are not to do anything that is uncomfortable; that the old theories and rules are wrong; that you must just stand comfortably in front of the ball and hit it. There is only one thing—one tiny little thing; and that is the position of your little toe. If you are standing right, and have your little toe in an easy, natural, and free position, the ball cannot help going straight. Swinging does not matter, hitting hardly matters. " Just attend to the little toe," the writer seems to say, " and see that it is comfortable and doing what it likes, and the ball must get up of itself off the tee, and fly to the green, and drop into the hole." And then he adds : " But if the beginner finds that he plays better with the toe in a stiff position, then he had better not attempt at present to adopt what is, nevertheless, the only natural, logical, and scientific method of golf."

The time comes when the beginner must put some at least of these theories into practice ; when having got the professional, in whose hands he is supposed to have placed himself, safely out of the way, and bought a really good driver at a shop in the Haymarket, he puts a new ball on the tee and prepares light-heartedly to enjoy himself. It is then, of course, that the baleful influence of the experts begins to assert itself. He addresses the ball and wonders if he is in a natural position, or, finding he is not, decides on one or other of the many stances laid down, and realises for the first time that it has not occurred to any of the book-writers to publish photographs of the ball and the club as they look from the player's point of view, instead of from the onlooker's. He fixes his eye on the white ball and, as the club swings back, all that he has ever read on the subject rushes through his mind.

I suppose there is no moment so packed with pure mental processes as that occupied by the swing back of the beginner's club. Pages and pages of printed matter flash across his mind like a line off a reel. When the club is shoulder-high he has decided to take Taylor's advice; and when it is at the top of the swing he thinks that perhaps Braid is safer for a beginner; as he begins to come down he thinks of Vaile, and tries to remember what it was he said. And so packed with thought has been this second or two that it appears to him like an agony that has been endured for months and must be ended somehow, and that instantly, lest he sink under the torture of it. And somehow in the final swing, or rather tumbledown of the club, he remembers with a guilty pang that all is not as it should be with his little toe. There is a horrible concussion, and the ball is seen lying twenty yards away to the left.

It is then, from these dreadful birth-throes, that the true golfer begins to be born. He snatches up his clubs and runs after the ball as though it might escape his vengeance, determined only upon one thing, to hit it, and to hit it far away, mentally registering a vow that should he miss it he will go home. He runs up to it, seizes an iron club, and, without any thought of stance or address, strikes it, strikes it hard in anger; and lo, with a click and a song in the air the ball flies up and away, straight and true, now a grey dot against the sky, now a running and bouncing white spot on the green slope a hundred and fifty yards ahead. The murderous anger in his face is smoothed out into a happy smile; he says to himself, " I will do that again." And he goes up to the ball and smites once into the air and then digs up a pound and a half of turf. Then he gives it up, and does not care how he hits; and once more the ball mounts like a lark, and drops a yard away from the hole, into which it is rolled by the beginner's lucky putt. "Down in six," says his companion in congratulatory terms; but in the private register of his mind the beginner marks it as three, and feels that with a little more care he might have done it in two. And when he has done that his feet have entered upon the road that has no end.

The golf professional is often a curious person. He may have been a member of the artisan class who has begun life as a caddie, and who, probably to the grief of his parents, refused to forsake the links for any more disciplined and regular occupation; who nevertheless has survived physically and morally the loafing years of caddieship, who has worked in a desultory way at clubmaking, or rather club assembling, who has shown a definite aptitude for the game and gained an entrance into the envied ranks of the " plus " men, and who has ultimately got permanent employment as a professional at a golf club. I am not speaking now of course, of the brilliant few who have achieved at some time or other the open championship, but of the ordinary working professionals who are unknown to anything but a local fame. It is these men who are responsible for the so-called teaching of nine golfers out of ten; and a more haphazard, inefficient business it would be hard to find. To the innocent beginner there is something magical in the word " professional " : it is held to imply a knowledge of all the mysteries of the most mysterious game in the world ; and because the professional can himself play the game, it is taken for granted that he can also teach it. I have before me six books on golf, all written by professionals ; and each book, in the part devoted to an attempt to expound the proper methods of learning the game, contains the advice "Put yourself in the hands of your professional."

Of every ten people who begin to play the game of golf I suppose that five pick it up for themselves, and arrive, by natural aptitude and practice, at a form which represents pretty well their full capability in the matter. Of the other five, perhaps one will seriously look until he finds a really efficient teacher, and so in time achieve a good style and a decent game ; the other four confidingly "place themselves in the hands of their professional," and either give up the game in disgust as a consequence or else spend the rest of their golfing life as con-firmed slicers, toppers, founderers, and more or less contented foozlers. I know it is a serious thing to say a word in criticism of a body of men who are held in almost superstitious esteem ; who are, moreover, for the most part, very decent, agreeable fellows. But I do seriously say that the average professional, considered as a teacher of golf —which is one of the things which he professes—is a complete though probably unconscious fraud.

Let us consider what happens to the golfer who "places himself in the hands of his professional." You may see him about the links in these early spring days, accompanied by this same professional

E   65

and a caddie carrying a very new and expensive bag heavily stocked with clubs. For the first thing a professional does is " to fit you out with a bag of clubs." A part of his living, of course, is derived from these sales, and if he did his business competently he would be much the best person to act as a beginner's adviser and provider. But he understands the business of selling no better than the business of teaching. Instead of selling his victim one club at a time, and teaching him the use of that club and making him able to play with it, and so producing such confidence that the learner feels that it is these clubs, and these alone, with which he can play, he loads him at once with a full assortment of mysterious implements. " Let me see," he says, estimating the enthusiasm and purse of the victim with a hungry eye, " you will want a driver, and a brassie to match it." He selects one of these ; but the victim, preferring the polish and finish of another one, indicates a faint preference for that. " Yes, that's a good club, too." says the professional, and allows him to make his own ignorant choice. " Then you will want a cleek "—the poor wretch will not want it, and probably will soon earnestly desire to be without it—" and an iron, and a mashie, and a putter."

The one club that a beginner probably wants to possess is a niblick, for he is attracted and reassured by its large surface. This is also chosen for him, and he feels that he is complete. " There's a beautiful club," says the professional, handing him a driving mashie ; " you can get a very long, straight ball with that." And as the learner wishes to

get long, straight balls he buys it. "Then you
want a jigger for running up," says the professional,
"and on this course a baffy is very useful; in
fact you must have it on this course. You won't
want any more clubs." With a pair of gloves, a
tin of some adhesive substance, and a box of balls,
the victim sallies forth to the first tee, feeling that
the battle is more than half won.

He makes several attempts to hit the ball with
his driver; the professional gives him a few simple
directions, and tells him to take it easy, and not
try to hit the ball too hard. The first time that
he misses it he is told that he took his eye off it;
the second, that he raised his head; the third
that he moved his body; the fourth, that he came
down on it; the fifth, that he took his eye off it;
the sixth, that he fell over on to it; the seventh,
that he took his eye off it; the eighth, that he
went back too quick; and the ninth, that he took
his eye off it. How the professional could be sure
of this, seeing that at the moment the stroke was
made he was interestedly watching an approach
shot by a scratch player, it is difficult to know;
but the victim takes his word for it. The professional then himself takes the club, and saying,
"You want to do it more like this," drives with
lightning rapidity a very satisfactory and agreeable
ball straight away for some two hundred and
twenty yards. He likes it so much that he does
another, and another; the sensation of driving new
balls off the tee being one which custom has not
staled even for the jaded professional. "Do it
more like that," he says, and reluctantly surrenders

the club into the hands of the beginner, who by this time, stimulated by admiration and the appearance of ease with which it is done, is thirsting to have another lunge at it.

A heavily socketed stroke, accompanied by a faint crack, sends the ball about thirty yards to the extreme left. The professional picks up the driver and examines its heel. "I am afraid you have done for it," he says; "you came right down on it." The fracture of the driver is beyond a doubt. "I can put a new head on it," says the professional, "but of course it won't be the same club. I tell you what I will do; you had better have another driver, and I will fix this one up for you so that you can play with it, and keep it as a second one. Now I think we had better try some brassie shots." The same process is gone through again, all except the breaking of the club. Perhaps by this time the learner is showing some dawning ability to hit the ball; but he never knows why he hits it. The professional never tells him that, although it is the only thing worth knowing and learning at golf.

There may be any one of a hundred reasons why he fails to hit the ball, but if he does get it fairly, it is because he is doing something right; it is that something which it is so important he should know. The pupil's grip, his stance, position of his body and shoulders, the action of his left arm and wrist are all wrong; and as he makes stroke after stroke the teacher draws attention now to one, now to another of these defects; he never addresses himself to one at a time in order to get it right. And just as the pupil is getting dimly to understand some of the first principles of handling one club, he is put on to another that requires quite different treatment, so his mistakes begin all over again. At the end of the lesson he retires with an aching body and a collection of hacked and gashed balls, and with an understanding that if he would learn to play golf, he must repeat this process continually with the professional, and "stick at it." He does stick at it until he is weary. The professional, feeling that there are no more sales to be effected, grows weary also, and departs to some new victim. By this time the learner is convinced that it is his clubs that are wrong, and goes secretly by himself to a shop and buys new ones. He is ashamed to be seen by the professional playing with them, so he avoids him ; and this is one of the many reasons why the professional is a bad business man.

The teaching of a thing is a science quite different from the performance of it. As a rule only a man can teach a thing who has either learned it or who has thoughtfully analysed and discovered the principles which govern his instinctive and natural doing of it. But the ordinary golf professional is equipped in neither way. Poor teacher, how can he teach who never learned ? He picked his golf up as a little boy, in the bright sunshine of some seaside links, trudging through the bents with the other ragamuffins, with the noise of the sea in his ears and the wind in his face ; he never thought how the thing was done, he just did it. And now that he is making a living out of his ability to do it, he is called upon out of his own knowledge and experience so to converse with some stiff, middle-aged, sedentary gentleman that he also will be able to do it. No wonder that such teaching is a failure. You might as well ask some peasant from a vineyard on the banks of the Rhone to teach French in an English academy of young ladies. The golf links of Great Britain are studded with the results of such teaching. You may recognise them anywhere—men playing stiffly, awkwardly, and anxiously, with the hands far apart, the left arm bent like a bow, the club overswung till it is pointing almost to the ground, the heels of their drivers marked as though with a punch. They are happy or unhappy, according to temperament, but what they are playing is not golf.

Only they who have learned can teach.

Springtime in London

PERHAPS you have forgotten it already,
that sudden breath of the warm south-west
that came and told us that Winter was
over. For all of us there is a moment in
every year when we receive this first message of
the returning Spring; somewhere it comes and
find us, and takes us by surprise. To one it will
come in the form of a sunbeam that strikes at a new
angle into a dusky room; to another it will appear
in the colour of a strip of sky seen between crowded
roofs; to another in the reflection of light from a
puddle on the ground. But everything living feels
it and knows it—the prisoner in the prison, the
seaman on the ship, the engine-driver suddenly
rounding a curve and feeling amid the steam and
dust and clatter that he has entered a sweeter world
—creeping things and flying things, and perhaps
even the fishes in the sea. The day on which this
message comes to us is one of the great days of the
year, greater even than that day in January when
we first realise that the afternoons are lengthening
and that the sun is coming back to us again. And
as when a friend returns to his kindred after a long
absence, or a monarch to his country, we make it a
day of festival, should we not make a little celebration, even if it be only in words, of the return of

Spring? Believe me, it requires a little courage to write about Spring, or about any of the familiar miracles that are commonplaces with us ; there is nothing new to say about them. But when we perform a ceremony we do not invent new things to say ; we repeat old forms of words that are hallowed by association with the occasion celebrated. Hence the outcrop of verses in the poets' corners of the newspapers—an annual ceremony like the breaking of the lilac buds and unfolding of the almond blossom ; and hence this tribute to the first breeze of Spring.

I think it was Mr. George Moore who said that the constant temptation of the writer was to go and see someone—to look for an external stimulus instead of the one within his own breast. But there is another temptation for anyone whose work is done indoors, and that is simply to go out, not in search of a stimulus, but for the sheer pleasure of being out-of-doors. To this temptation I succumbed one morning. At a time when I should have been busy working I shamelessly gave up and, answering the pleading of two small very bright brown eyes, went for a walk in Hyde Park, accompanied by about fifteen inches of leaping, barking insanity. And it was there in the broad undulating fields sacred to babies and dogs that I met the breath from the south-west which told me that Winter was a thing of the past. It was a promise ; rough weather would still come ; March would bring its gales and April its cold rains and biting winds, but the main forces of Winter were broken up and scattered, and the armies of the

Spring and the Summer were already on the march.
There was the advance guard, the crocuses in
battalions of gold and purple and white already
occupying the grass which a little while ago was
deep with snow. And I was not the only one to
feel the promise. The dogs barked and raced;
great ripples spread and fled over the grass before
the breath of the warm wind; even the babies in
their carriages lolled and slumbered with blander
stupefaction than usual; and down by the Serpen-
tine, which a fortnight ago was a sheet of ice and
iron, little warm wavelets lapped and laughed
against the shore, and the waterfowl in their island
home screamed and gobbled and splashed as
though the business of the year had begun in
earnest. Over in Whitehall, Ministers and miners
were discussing the tremendous and fateful issue
of the day; I could not help thinking that if they
could all have come out and sat in the sun in the
Park, and talked it over there, the idea of a coal
strike would have struck them all as an absurdity.

Insanity demanding that I should throw sticks
for it to a great distance in order that they should
be rapidly retrieved, I for some time devoted
myself to that business. Then I became involved
in a canine dispute concerning the rights of treasure-
trove in a partially eaten india-rubber ball. The
settlement of this to the satisfaction of all concerned
took some time, and when I turned to go the
morning had clouded over, as our London mornings
will, and the mysterious whisper of promise was no
longer in the wind. But the promise had been
given; in earnest of it the crocuses lay there still,

a golden payment on account of riches to come ;
and I returned in the faith and knowledge that
nothing had happened to the miraculous machinery,
and that all the lovely and inevitable wonders of
the year would really come again.

Monte Carlo Revisited

IN one respect, and in one only, Monte Carlo is like heaven : it is assumed that everyone wishes to go there, and that everyone who is at all able to, does go there. It stands as a kind of symbol of the desirable ; and if at this time of year you say to anyone " I am going to Monte Carlo," the countersign is invariably " Lucky dog ! " And to the credit of Monte Carlo it must be admitted that one's own sensations on setting forth for it are not unsuitably described in those words. It is the first holiday of the year, and it expresses our impatience to rush to meet the returning Spring, instead of waiting for it in England. Certainly the setting out is fun. The sight of the Mediterranean express at Calais, with the long lines of brown sleeping-cars with their polished lettering and magic label " Calais—Vintimille," is agreeable ; it is fun to wander up and down the corridors and see what acquaintances you have among the travellers ; it is even fun to resume your acquaintance with the interior domestic economy of the august corporation in the spelling of whose name sixty-three gunmetal letters are employed ; to wonder what " tisane sleeping-car " is like, and what dread potion is designated by the word " grog." Some day I intend to tear down this veil, but I postpone it because one must keep some mysteries in the world, and if these two were gone I should feel that the possibilities of life had been diminished for me. It is delicious to open one's window in the early morning somewhere near Orange or Avignon, and to get the first breath of the cool and tranquil airs and smell the perfumes of another Spring. And best of all it is to wake up on one's first morning in Monte Carlo, to go out on the balcony in the hot sunshine and look out over the peacock shallows and the turquoise depths of the Mediterranean, to stroll in the garden among scents of lemon and stock and roses and geranium and verbena, to eat the tiny sweet oranges warm off the trees, and to realise that the sun shines and that you have no work to do. That first morning is really the best thing that Monte Carlo has to give you, and perhaps the best way to taste its pleasures would be to spend but one night there and, if by any chance the first morning was not fine, to return as far as Marseilles or Lyons and make a fresh descent upon it, and so procure a full indulgence of its delicious surprise.

But beyond that, and your first luncheon in one of its exquisite restaurants, Monte Carlo ceases to live quite up to its reputation. I feel a certain diffidence about suggesting that there can be any qualification of the virtues of a place from which I have just returned, and to which everyone who has not been there would like to go. But it is six years since I was there last, and will probably be as long before I am there again; and though I am capable of the keenest enjoyment, I do begin to think that Monte Carlo is something of a delusion. One is supposed to " cast care to the winds " when there, and one pictures a society of free, careless, happy people, gay and beautiful, laughing and enraptured, moving to enchanted music about the flower-perfumed terraces of this azure shore. What one does see is a haggard, dissipated, careworn crowd blinking in a sunshine which is obviously afflicting to their fevered brows ; a crowd for the most part of unsightly Teutonic people whose grey and shabby ranks are but slightly leavened by the trim and cool-looking English and American visitors. The people who enjoy Monte Carlo best are those who do not live in the place itself but in the villas surrounding it ; and as my host was among these fortunate few I was able to enjoy the beauty, and avoid the sordidness of Monte Carlo. For there, the word has slipped out ; Monte Carlo is on the whole a sordid place. It is obvious that it must be so, since the crudest form of gambling is the central pulse of its life ; but it seems a pity. I can attain to no heights of moral indignation about gambling ; if people like to amuse themselves that way, it is all one to me ; and I share the common frailties of the gambler in feeling a fool when I lose, and extraordinarily clever and far-sighted when I win. But most of the time there is no real gambling at Monte Carlo. People play desperately with what they can well afford to lose, and the people who can't afford to lose take care as a rule not to gamble. You see millionaires toiling for hours at some system by which they must risk at least ten times what they stand to

win, and having won perhaps fifty pounds after a
hard day's work, rising haggard but exultant from
the table. Or you see some fortunate being with
a practically unlimited credit at the Bank who
has taken his twenty louis to play with and lost
them, enjoying all the sensations of the ruined man
and telling you with rather a tragic air of finality
that he has not got a five-franc piece left with
which to buy a drink. And to-morrow he goes to
the Bank and draws another fifty pounds and goes
through the same performance. "Come and play
golf to-morrow morning," you say. "I am afraid
I can't, old chap," he answers. "I am rather
down, and I have got to go and work to get it
back." And he does work; and his work consists
of sitting at a green table with knitted brows, with
a pile of money and a little card covered with
calculations in front of him, and watching his
money raked away into the bottomless tills of the
Bank.

All this is play and make-believe, of course. For
most of the players the coins are mere counters,
although they happen to be made of gold instead
of brass. There is only one law which I am quite
sure of with regard to this form of gambling; and
that is that if you want the money very much, are in
real need of it and could make good use of it, you
will not get it. It would hardly be fair if you did.
Money that does good is not got in that way.
The wrong kind of courage is needed to win. One
of the many reasons, apart from a purely mathe-
matical one, that the Bank wins so enormously is
that people exhibit plenty of courage when they

are losing, and none at all when they are winning. The loser goes on increasing his stakes without a tremor until his last coin is gone; but the winner gets timid, and instead of holding on to a big chance in the strength of his winnings, rushes about hither and thither over all the chances, until his winnings have melted away again.

One of the chief disappointments of Monte Carlo is that this commerce in coin, superficial and make-believe though it is—for though people come hoping to make money, they come prepared to lose it—produces an atmosphere of sordidness and ugliness which does not mingle at all well with the extravagant daintiness and sumptuousness and luxury of the stage which it envelops. The public gambling rooms with their preposterously extravagant decorations are in the crowded hours a really most unpleasant place, with their hot atmosphere and their ill-dressed throng of ugly and covetous people. The so-called private rooms of the *Cercle des Étrangers* are exactly the same, except that the ugly people are richer and wear more finery; while the rooms of the Sporting Club, which are supposed to be reserved for the élite, and are in fact open to practically everybody who cares enough to take the slight trouble involved in gaining admission to them, reveal the nicest people in the most unbecoming light. If gambling is such fun —and I dare say it is, under certain conditions—it ought surely to be possible to make it pretty to look at, especially when pretty people are engaged in doing it; but it is really quite the ugliest amuse-ment from the point of view of an onlooker that can be imagined. It is very banal to say all this ; I had quite hoped to discover something charming and attractive in what attracts so many others ; and as I didn't, perhaps I should say no more about it.

Doubtless one of the charms of the whole world of Monte Carlo is its extreme unreality, and a Londoner who has never seen it would form the best idea of it if he imagined the crowd in the Park on Ascot Sunday transferred to the White City on a hot summer morning. Even the innocent flowers look expensive and unreal, and Mont Agel is like a painted background. You come upon a church in Monte Carlo with a sense of impropriety ; and such a reality as death is so out of place that it is not only never mentioned, but it is so kept in the background as to foster the illusion that it does not exist. And yet I had an experience coming away which seemed to summarise the whole spirit of the place. I had left my friends poring over the tables in the Sporting Club, and had come down to the station, which is on the very edge of a cliff, so that you can look down over the platform railings to the sea breaking below. A storm came suddenly up from the sea that afternoon ; the bay was covered with white horses, and a strong wind from the south sang on the exposed platform. Suddenly there was a rush to the railings ; and we saw that there was a man in the water about five hundred yards from the shore. No boat was in sight ; he must have been in a boat which had capsized. He was lying on his back evidently trying to husband his strength and let himself be floated in to the shore; but there was a big sea in the bay, and every quarter of a minute a white crest foamed over his head, while his body was tossed about like a piece of wet cloth. Somebody telephoned down to the harbour, but we knew that it would be at least a quarter of an hour before the fastest boat could reach him, and he had obviously been in the water for some time, and must have been nearly spent. We, who looked on, sick with horror and pity, could do nothing. The cliff was steep-to, and the strongest swimmer in the world would have had the life dashed out of him if he had tried to swim out from its foot where the heavy seas were breaking on the rocks. So we stood looking, while the little arms attached to the wet sop that was a centre of human agony waved themselves about, and sea after sea flung itself easily and heavily on their poor efforts. And in the middle of it all the train de luxe arrived, and amid cries of " *En voiture, messieurs !* " and the hoisting of luggage through windows, and the identification of jealously reserved places, the general attention was diverted. There was no time to see him sink and die, and he would never be rescued. The sun came out from behind a cloud and flooded the sea, turning it to a milky-green and, as the train moved out, illuminated the last mouse-like struggles of the drowning man. Three hundred yards above me they were calmly intent on the spinning of the roulette-wheel; three hundred yards below me a man was being so inconsiderate as to spoil the view of the sea by dying in it—an act so unusual that there was no apparatus either for saving him or tidying him up; and about me were voices disputing about the occupancy of certain peacock-plush compartments.

The train ran under the tunnel and out again into the sun, and the whole thing was gone. What happened to the man I knew, but would never hear. What happened to the others I might hear, but would never know. Wise men fight against chance and play with certainties; behind me beyond the hill the play was with chance, and the fight against certainty. I thought it a highly charac-teristic, if somewhat dramatic, ending to a week in Monte Carlo.

The London Season

IT is some time ago now since those scribes whose singular duty it is to chronicle the doings of the social world discovered with alarm that the season was about to " collapse." Here was a pretty how-do-you-do. Rushing hither and thither in the commotion of one kind or another which is their element, they had observed that something was amiss with the foundations of their world ; and suddenly discovering that there were at least two dates in July on which no " important " social function was to take place, they became apprehensive as to the security of the whole social fabric, and brayed out their fears above the general uproar.

The truth was that they had deceived themselves. The art of making a fuss about things in print, of creating a social commotion in ink and type, had been cultivated by them with so much success, that they were blinded, like the squid, by their own discharges ; and the season was half-way through before they discovered that the brilliancy and splendour which they had been so busy describing had not existed at all, save in their own otherwise empty heads. So long ears were pricked forward, and loud braying voices declared that the season had collapsed.

Now that the secret is out, it may not be un-interesting to consider some of the changes which have taken place in what is called the London season. It has certain structural features in which there is little change from year to year. The public part of it consist of certain race meetings, operas, flower shows, tournaments, and charity functions, which are annual fixtures, and in which a large portion of society is concerned. These things occupy the newspapers, and are the occasion of a certain amount of that bustle, spectacle, and money-spending of which the commotion of social life consists.

But what makes a season really memorable, and gives it a hall-mark of its own, is the degree of success attained in quite private functions. There are a dozen houses in Mayfair and St. James's—perhaps half a dozen—which can make or mar a season from this point of view, by giving or withholding the kind of entertainment in which the many circles that form London Society may touch one another and revolve round the same sun. Entertainments of this kind are purely formal and not intimate ; and they are rapidly falling into disfavour. It is the almost total absence of them, I think, which has made some recent seasons such very unbrilliant affairs. Commotion and rush there have been ; but they have been un-distinguished commotion, and rush which is merely the normal affliction of the idle world raised to a higher point. People are becoming more and more shy of entertaining on the grand and formal scale.

One reason for this undoubtedly is that society is becoming less and less patient of formality of any kind. In its clothes, in its manners, in its speech, and in the things which really amuse it, the tendency is to become more free and easy, more impulsive, more impromptu. People prefer to meet in small gatherings at short notice, and do whatever amuses them most, rather than fix a distant date for some formal function which, when it comes will be voted a bore and a nuisance. Moreover, entertaining even on a grand scale, is a domestic affair transacted by a family in its own house. And functions in which a family unites to do anything at all are becoming more and more difficult to arrange. Different members of the family have their different sets of friends and different occupations; they are not interested in the same things or the same people. The greatly increased independence of young people, and the highly organised machinery which exists for their separate amusement, has made it difficult to get them to regard family functions of any kind at all seriously.

But there is another reason. Entertaining in the way I have described requires hostesses of a certain age and dignity, and with a social gift for carrying a great many people in their minds, and keeping in touch both with the new and old inhabitants of the social world. And people like this are disappearing. What happens to them I do not know; but there is now hardly anyone in London old enough to entertain in the way I have described. The hostesses grow younger and younger. For a season or two, when their daughters come out, they unwillingly play the part of the fond parent, and stand publicly revealed as such; but once the daughters are safely married they revert to their own youthful condition, cultivate their own special friends, wear smaller and smaller hats and shorter and shorter dresses, and remain at whatever age is fashionable. Just at present nearly all the hostesses in London are between thirty and thirty-five; and people whom I seem to remember a few years ago as kind elderly ladies now look at me coyly from under tea-cosy hats, and are to be seen with some special faithful male friend at operas or picture shows, thrilling once again to the dawn of emotion, and discovering anew what a wonderful thing life is. It would be absurd to ask such people to stand at the head of a staircase for four hours, saying the right and tactful thing to everybody. It would be cruel to snatch them from their new-found joys; cruel to take them away from the freedom and independence which they seem to be tasting for the first time, and require dull, domestic, and social duties of them. You see one of them, perhaps at the wedding of her grandson, and it is remarked how beautiful is her devotion and fidelity to some portly Cabinet Minister. " Isn't it too divine the way she has stuck to him—and he is so dull," is the world's comment upon one of these perennial romances ; and no one seems to think it funny or even at all unusual.

This total refusal to grow old on the part of women in society cannot but have its effect on the whole social machinery, and has not a little to do with the changes that have been observed in the London season. In the true social fabric a woman at a certain age sinks her individuality and becomes the centre of something, represents something. Now people represent merely themselves and seem, like rival tradesmen, to disclaim any connection with anyone else of the same name. It is every one for himself or herself in society nowadays, and Mrs. Grundy takes the hindmost. Another reason for the change is in the part played by Royalty. The King and Queen have shown a very definite conception of where their own social duties lie, and it is not the conception of the world that lives entirely for amusement.

Certainly if there is to be a season at all, the more brilliant and interesting it can be made the better. If its only obvious result is that it takes twenty minutes to drive from Hyde Park Corner to Piccadilly Circus, if there is merely to be an increase of the insane rush and exhaustion without pleasure, it is apt to become a very considerable nuisance. The truth is that when people lived quietly in the country for seven months in the year and came to London for three, there was some truly social result of the London season ; but now, when nobody stays anywhere for more than four days, and people who live in the country are continually running up to London, and people who live in London are continually rushing down to the country, there is very little sense or meaning in it at all.

The Silly Season

EVERY year, when Parliament rises; when the leaves of the town trees begin to turn brown and dusty; when the blinds are down in the great town houses and the furniture swathed in holland, and the caretakers' cats sun themselves in fashionable streets; when great business houses are in that condition of somnolence known as "slack"; when the very churches are only half in commission; when clubs migrate and theatres are empty, and the great chef of the fashionable restaurants gives place to his assistant, and all the deans, comedians, officials, actor-managers, politicians, peers and chorus girls whose doings and sayings supply the world in serious moments with its staple food for thought and debate, are out of town; when the serious season of balls and dinner parties and amusements comes to an end, then the silly season begins.

And what is the silly season, whose topics occupy the newspapers from August to mid-September? A scrutiny of our great journals during this period and a comparison of their contents then with their contents, say, in May or June, does not by any means explain the title; for by any sane estimate these contents are no whit sillier in August than they are in May; are less

silly, in fact. But they are less official. One of
the developments of journalism in the last ten years
has been certainly to increase the importance of
officialism in England. In the newspaper offices
every public man is catalogued as being " good
for " certain subjects. There are a few privileged
people, like Charlie Chaplin, who are heard on
every subject, and who, if they utter the simplest
platitude, will hear it banging up and down the
columns of the Press for a week afterwards. But as
a general rule it is one man one topic ; and when
these topics " come up " the appropriate man
is telegraphed to or interviewed for an opinion.
Then there is the great officialism of Parliament
which absorbs so much of the ordinary stuff of
news ; there are the official preachers and actors,
whose doings and sayings form part of the daily
official information ladled out to the public. But
when all these people go away from London and
cease from their official functions, the newspapers
are thrown back on the ordinary affairs of life for
their news. Quite human and interesting facts
are recorded, and quite important questions
discussed, for which no space could be afforded
while news was still official. In to-day's paper, for
example, I find a most interesting account of the
British Museum watch cat, and its method of
ejecting dogs from the precincts of that institution
—a piece of knowledge which I could probably have
gained only in the silly season. Instead of long
columns about charity balls and the costumes
worn thereat, instead of verbatim reports of endless
speeches in which insincere men speak something

other than the truth at great length, one has reasonably brief reports of the natural and unofficial doings of plain people all over the world ; that is, instead of accounts of dull things, one reads accounts of interesting things. There comes a sudden expansion and broadening of the mind of the newspaper which cannot but be refreshing to anyone who reads it for the purpose for which it was originally designed—that is, to give the news. If you would know how a people are really living, you will not read the accounts of their Parliaments and the movements of their Courts, but the small items of information which in the French papers are called *faits divers*, and are in truth facts, various and far-gathered, which teach you not how the ten thousand, but how the twenty million are living.

But there is another feature of the silly season which is more commonly recognised, and that is the correspondence on some purely humane subject to which the newspapers open their columns at this time. In the younger days of our era it was things like the sea-serpent which occupied the August correspondence. But we have got a little further than that ; and the subject which now most commonly occupies us is some form or other of the great woman question ; whether women are selfish or not, whether they are better-looking than they used to be, whether they make as good wives as they used to make, whether marriage is a failure, and if so, why ? These and kindred topics are now the common material of the silly season. Well, when all is said and done, all of them are of perennial interest, and some of them of the first importance to the human race. I do not profess to read these discussions, but an occasional glance at them seldom fails to reveal some interesting point of view, or some expression of quiet common sense that in the absence of other things, deemed more important, has managed to get itself uttered. One can only compare London newspapers with London streets at this time of year. In many of them, ordinarily filled with chaotic movement and haunted by endless clamour, there is at this time something approaching peace and silence. You can walk in a leisurely way and hear yourself think. And in the newspapers there is also a kind of peace and silence from the more blatant and strident voices; in the absence of which certain still small voices, which have a value and importance of their own, become audible for the first time. As a rule we do not hear them, so great is the overwhelming noise; and it is worth while staying behind for a little when that has passed, if only to be reminded of the quiet diapason of existence which is always sounding for those who have ears to hear it.

The Moabite's Holiday

I SUPPOSE that in the minds of the English people there is no idea so closely associated with the month of August as the idea of change. The month divides the year into two halves; it is the end of the half in which we look forward, the point in which outdoor life with us reaches its climax, and it is the beginning of that other and darker half, when we regretfully turn our backs upon sun and flowers and begin to go down into the valley of the year, with mists and fog and winter night at the end of it. In this respect the month does itself imply change, the most complete change, so far as our habits of life are concerned, of the whole year.

But when people talk of "going away for a change" they generally talk of something which does not really exist. If one takes a little trouble at this time of the year to observe the holiday habits of people, or goes to any of the principal places which holiday-makers frequent, one cannot help seeing how genuine and deep-seated is the average man's fear of change. The ordinary middle-class summer holiday is a thing of routine, convention, and habit. It is true that the governing idea with the majority who live in inland towns is to go to the sea and procure a change of air, and this is almost the only change actually achieved. People who frequent watering-places on the coast have really very little to do with the sea. It is there as a kind of background to existence; but it is a property sea, a thing to be waded or swum into for a few yards, whose blank horizon is agreeably suitable to a point of view which has vacancy for its background. For the rest, what does the average man seek in his so-called change? He comes from a crowded town; he betakes himself to a place where there are crowds. The "season" of Little Puddleton is not considered a success unless its strip of beach or promenade is actually thronged with visitors. More than this, the average holiday-maker of this class, fearful of anything unfamiliar or new, likes to go to the same place every year, and to be able, in the crowd with which he mingles, to recognise many habitués like himself—in short, to meet the same people year after year. He likes the same food that he gets in London, he reads the same newspapers, his amusements are the same—picture-palaces, concerts, music-halls, variety entertainments. He eats a little more, drinks a little more, smokes a little more, sleeps a little more, and thinks, if possible, a little less; that is the extent of his change. If you pay a visit at this time to such places as Brighton or Southend, you will see all this exemplified in the persons of thousands of Londoners of two distinct classes. Brighton's name of "London-by-the-Sea" is explanatory of its popularity with the well-to-do Londoner; his whole atmosphere is imported there to a world which is as familiar to him as Piccadilly. To another class Southend means exactly the same thing. It is crowded, and it is familiar; and therefore they seek it when they go for a change.

The more one considers the habit of holiday-making the more does one realise how little use is made of real change as a restorative and recreative influence. People whose whole lives are a holiday —or might be if they knew how to take one— hardly ever get any real change. The same little world moves from London to Carlsbad, or Vichy, or Aix, or some other foreign watering-place, where its settled habits are provided for; and from there to Scotland and from Scotland onwards to pay various visits. The same people are encountered in the same houses, living the same kind of life, surrounded by the same circumstances. Then people, servants, motor-cars, photographs, and table toys are all carted wholesale to the south of France; and from there return to the country, or to London, or move backwards and forwards between the two—always the same kind of food, the same servants, the same books and newspapers to read, the same people to talk to. All this may sound very material, and it may be said that these are but the mere clothing and externals of ourselves, and that it is no more absurd to carry them with us than it is to take with us the kind of clothing to which we are accustomed. But if you consider how large a part of any life such things must mean —and they almost entirely fill and occupy some lives—you will see how desirable it is to import some little change and variety into them. When I see people with large yachts which are, except for a fortnight in the year, chiefly at anchor in the Solent ; with motor-cars whose chief mileage is covered in carrying the chauffeur between a house in London and a house in the country ; with freedom to do as they like, which seems to be employed almost entirely in doing things which they protest are a boredom, I think, perhaps quite wrongly, what wonderful uses I could make of such machinery. My yacht should not take me to Cowes or to Deauville, but to the Baltic or the Adriatic, to wander amid the isles of Greece, or the Sounds of Scandinavia ; my motor-cars would carry me, not on any routine path of habit, but along the broad roads of Europe, not on any fixed plan, but as the fancy took me ; and my freedom should be used in wandering, and seeing, and comprehending, and always consciously choosing. There are people who have both the means and the sense to live like this, but the world that is written about in newspapers sees or knows little of them.

The truth is that deep in the heart of ordinary men and women lies a great dislike, a positive fear of change. Change implies trouble to the mind and fatigue and possible discomfort to the body. Discomfort—is it not the bogey that is waiting for us all as middle-age approaches, which at heart we really fear far more than real danger and real distresses ? How many things do we cease to do or abstain from doing because they are uncomfortable ? How many of the limited experiences we do achieve are only acceptable on the condition that they are made quite comfortable and easy for us? It is less trouble and more comfortable to sit in an arm-chair with a book than to take a walk through East End streets on a stormy night; no trouble at all is required to extract a certain amount of interest from the one; a great deal of trouble and fatigue is required to discover the larger interest that may lie in the other. Strange sights, strange food, strange wines, strange music, strange points of view are not really acceptable to the ordinary person in whom curiosity is dead. Not only are they unacceptable, but they have no chance of being acceptable; the fact that they are strange is enough to shut them away from his experience. And it is so with the whole of life, although, since the dimension of time is fixed for us, the only way in which we can expand our lives is by filling them with change and variety of experience.

It is in this way that so many people make failures of their lives, or, in the words of the Psalmist, " change their glory into the similitude of an ox that eateth grass." And the ordinary holiday-maker, in his total lack of enterprise in this matter, and in his apparent fear of change and its results, seems to be very much in the case of Moab, according to Jeremiah, that gloomy prophet : " *Moab hath been at ease from his youth, and he hath settled on his lees, and hath not been emptied from vessel to vessel, neither hath he gone into captivity ; therefore his taste hath remained in him, and his scent is not changed.*"

A Night Journey

I HAVE an angel who bears me up when I set forth upon a journey; who transforms my experience, and sees to it that I do not dash my feet against the stone of dullness. Sense of Adventure, or whatever you may like to call him, he is probably some near relation to that angel of Make-believe who accompanies us through our childhood, and with whom most of us part company far too soon. Perhaps he is only that angel grown a little older and more diffident, no longer so intimate a part of our lives, and not always sure of a welcome; but whoever he is, he has the power to make many commonplace things interesting and even exciting. I am especially sure of finding him waiting for me at railway-stations and at the quay-sides of sea-ports. The other night circumstances ordained that I should rise from my comfortable chair by the fire, lay aside my after-dinner pipe, and set forth for the country of Scotland. Now, however glad I might be to arrive, the business of getting there seemed, on this stormy winter night, an inconvenient and even formidable affair. I summoned my angel, but he did not appear, and I had to set out alone in a taxicab.

I am one of those who can never set out on a

journey without a sensation of disturbance and depression. Many and far as my journeys have been, my heart sinks when it comes to the moment of getting up and going. Free as we may imagine ourselves to be, our existence always and everywhere runs on rails; if it is only for a few days we still must go on the track defined for us by circumstance, and when we change our destination or remove ourselves, we go through the process of switching ourselves off to some other track. And though I may be only going away for a few days, if my journey is to be any distance at all I look round my room ere I depart with a sense that something has come to a period, and may or may not be resumed. True, there are no great affairs to be adjusted or interests to be provided for when I move. My preparations can be very easily and simply made. But I feel when I set forth, and I know it is a feeling commonly shared, as though I were not only taking myself up by the roots, but also doing considerable damage to the soil in which they have been imbedded.

I had this feeling to a full degree as I drove through that part of London which for so many of us is associated with journeys to the North. There is a street called Goodge Street, through which one invariably drives on these occasions; I have never noticed it at any other time, but I believe it to be the most gloomy thoroughfare in the world, and it is certainly the one in which the sinking sensation becomes extreme. But having made the passage of Goodge Street I felt that there was no turning back, and that I must indeed launch myself. And although it cannot be called a hardship to go to bed in a modern railway train, and may, as things go, be accounted by some standards an almost extravagant luxury, yet if you regard it merely as a way of passing the night, it is not really a pleasant thing to be in a bed that shakes and jerks, and swings violently from side to side, and lurches and vibrates, and has, a foot or two beneath it, an iron machinery of wheels that groans and hums loudly in various keys throughout the night. To be made to sleep in such a bed in an ordinary house would be regarded as an ingenious form of torture. Nevertheless my spirits rose not a little when I entered the lighted orderliness of St. Pancras; for St. Pancras is a station with which I have only pleasant associations.

And let me tell you that it matters very much to the traveller who sets forth with these depressing sensations which station he departs from. Of all London railway stations Waterloo depresses me the most, and although the two longest journeys I have ever made began there, travel seems to me a sordid and petty business when I start from Waterloo. Euston has two associations in my mind—one, the dreary one of going back to everyday life after the paradise of youthful visits to London; the other, the more agreeable adventure of the Irish mail. King's Cross means Scotland or week-end visits. Paddington I associate entirely with Cornwall, for I never go up the river and I never go to race meetings. Victoria I associate with trivial journeys for trivial purposes;

Liverpool Street with chaos and sordid discomfort, ending in a headache and the green stupor of Suffolk; Charing Cross with the continent of Europe, and the sense of spending more money than I can afford. But St. Pancras was reserved for me almost entirely as the gateway to pleasant things, and the Midland Railway an organisation founded and conducted for the purpose of taking me to desirable places and people whom it makes me happy to see. Perhaps this is because I have used it so little in the past; but I shall try to use it more in the future.

Well, I found my angel waiting for me beside the long train; and as I had some time to spare, we walked up and down and looked at this strange articulated conveyance in which I was to be dragged out into the night. Only a little of it was devoted to the accommodation of people; the rest was parcel and mail vans, with gaping sides through which packages of every kind and shape were being passed. I noticed among other things some boxes containing grapes, consigned from a merchant in Covent Garden to a fruiterer in Glasgow; and I thought that I detected here a piece of canny Scotch economy. These, I said, are grapes which arrived early this morning at Covent Garden, which London has all day had the chance of buying and has not bought; now they are being sent to Glasgow in the hope that the Glasgow people will think they are entirely fresh. No doubt the Glasgow fruiterer made an arrangement with him of Covent Garden that he would take certain stock remaining unsold at the end of the day at a reduction ; and as people do not buy grapes in the middle of the night, no time would be wasted by their conveyance in this manner. I dare say this was all wrong ; but I am convinced that someone was getting the better of some-one else over those grapes, and that the only person who would really pay would be the person who ultimately bought them to eat. My angel further pointed out to me with what extraordinary care this train had been prepared ; although it was going out into the night to be hauled through a gale of sleet and snow, every coach had been cleaned and polished as though for an exhibition. And when the two great engines were backed on, they too were beautiful in ruddy paint and polished brass ; and although no gallery of spectators admired them, hours and hours had been spent in making them beautiful for their rush through the night. And then the mail carts came driving up, and the bags with their various destinations marked upon them were thrown into the vans ; and to see in imagination through the canvas fabric all the different handwritings, all the different subjects and purposes of the human brain that were thus being communicated to so many different kinds of people, to consider how many destinies would be affected by the contents of even one of those bags —to feel all this was to be imbued with a sense, not that one was embarking on a wearisome and uninteresting journey, but that one was taking part in a highly romantic adventure.

We crept stealthily out of the station, and immediately the gale began to hum and roar in the ventilators. I had some talk with the guard in his spacious apartment as to the road we were to travel, and marvelled not a little at the bulk and intricacy of the work that was to occupy him through the night, if none of the parcels and packages in his charge was to fail to reach its destination punctually. And presently I lay down and turned the light out and tried to go to sleep, although the beating of the wheels and the calling of the gale, and the shaking and swinging of my couch, kept me long awake. But almost pleasanter than sleep was the thought that I was lying more or less comfortably between linen sheets in a little bedroom, while so many attentive and strenuous forces were at work hurling me through the air at the speed of a rocket. I thought of the engine-drivers and firemen sweating in the open air among the grit and cinders in front of me, of the red glow of the fires shining up into the snowy air; of the signalmen reading and listening in their signal-boxes, those jewels of light with which the whole of the way was threaded. We passed through Melton Mowbray; and I thought of the foxes returning to their earths, of the hounds dreaming in the kennels, of the wonderful horses dozing and sighing in their sleep, and all the high passions of the chase sunk down to nothing while we thundered along by copse and cover. And so thinking, I fell farther and farther away towards unconsciousness, now made aware, by the sound of a voice echoing under some empty station roof, that we were momentarily at rest, now warned by the sense of time and by an increasing sense of cold that we were up on the high wild moors by Hawes or Kirkby Stephen.

And the last and most vivid picture I had was when at half-past five in the morning I looked out and found the train pulled up at the station of Hawick. It was dark and windy, and bitterly cold ; the town stood revealed by the feathers of steam and smoke that flourished above the mill chimneys in the frozen moonlight, and by the squares of yellow light that showed in every building where Scotch people were already getting up in the frosty darkness to begin a new day of labour. It was with some sense of thankfulness and with no further need of the angelic services, that after that vision I got back between the sheets of my warm bed.

A Morning at Ely

ONE Monday morning I played truant on my way back from a week-end in Norfolk, and escaped from the train for three morning hours to visit the cathedral of Ely. It is difficult to say why I should have had such a sense of truantry, but undoubtedly, as the train disappeared that should have been carrying me on to London, I walked forth into the town of Ely with that lightness of heart which in properly constituted people is associated with adventure and misdoing. The morning mists were lying white over the fens, and their chill touch and the autumnal smell in the air spoke sharply of the end of summer and the departure of the sun.

I walked up the unknown street towards the unknown cathedral with the confidence of an explorer approaching the North Pole by compass. I had never seen the cathedral, but its attraction was definite and strong; I could have found it blindfold, for in such a place all roads lead to the cathedral, as for centuries it has been the centre to which so many journeying feet, so many loads of material, so much treasure and so much piety have been drawn. A massive wall appeared on my right with a great arch in it filled with mist; I turned in at the arch and found myself in the elaborate peace of the close. And there suddenly on my left loomed something enormous. The mist cleared a little and revealed masses of grey masonry occupying an incredible bulk of the sky, but masonry so far without visible form. I walked along seeking for some gate of access, and as I looked up at the long buttresses, the soaring lantern, and the flowing curves of the window traceries, I had a sense of that extraordinary combination of magnitude and stability combined with aerial lightness which Winchester also produces—a suggestion that the cathedral is not planted in the ground, but afloat, like a great ship at anchor, in the green close. And looking up at the towering walls and at the confusing perspective of the pinnacles one could almost have sworn that the fabric moved a little, as though at the impulse of some unseen tide.

I was pleased, as one is always pleased by a discovery which can be interpreted in one's own favour, to learn afterwards that the Abbot Simeon, who was the original builder of the cathedral, was a brother of Bishop Walkelin of Winchester, where he had himself been Prior. So that the shiplike aspects of the two cathedrals and their many other points of resemblance may perhaps not be accidental.

At last I found an open door, and entering was aware of that sensation of dizziness which the confounding proportions of a great interior induce. That soon passed, and I began to wander about on the preliminary feat of pedestrianism which is necessary before one can begin to grasp the design of such a building. It was so early that I was practically alone, and felt as though I had boarded a great deserted treasure-ship and were exploring all her holds and cabins. Up and down the immense nave of thirteen bays, and before its glorious façade of arches superimposed in perfect proportion I marched unwearied; stopping to marvel at the great beauty of the Galilee porch with its trefoiled arches, the curling leafage of its capitals, and the elaborate dog-tooth ornament that had so patiently and so elaborately been cut to enrich the mouldings. I stood and looked up into the wonderful central dome or lantern—does any other English cathedral, except the modern St. Paul's, possess a central dome? —and considered what I had read of its engineering and of its romantic beginnings. For Ely, like so many of our cathedrals, which we think of as monuments of slow and solid labour, suffered once from the plague of jerry-building.

Such was the zeal of its founders; such was the wealth of treasure that was brought to it by long pilgrimage across the fens; such, I have no doubt, the pious haste on the part of the Benedictines to extend the very handsome business that was being done in the way of offerings at St. Etheldreda's shrine, that safety in the building was sacrificed to speed, with the result that the great central tower, which was part of Abbot Simeon's original design, fell down in 1322; and the third great period in the life of the fabric, which was to crown it with its distinctive loveliness, began.

The same kind of accident has happened at some time or another in almost every English cathedral, resulting often in the destruction of a glorious thing and the putting of something less glorious in its place. But at Ely the ruin of the central tower was perhaps a blessing in disguise. For when Alan of Walsingham set to work to clear away the debris of the piers of the tower, and saw the great open space left at the crossing, it occurred to him that a light octagonal tower supporting a lantern and spire could be evolved out of the ruins. The difficulty lay in the engineering, as is apparent even to the lay visitor who looks upward into the apex of that great octagon. Vaulting was impossible, for the width is over seventy feet, and nowhere outside of Spain had such a space been vaulted. Neither could there be a ceiling, for no beams of seventy feet could be obtained, or, if obtained, could safely have borne any weight. The solution at once poetic and daring, was found in the construction of an octagonal collar of wood from which eight posts could rise, forming a wooden lantern with vertical sides. The stonework was finished in six years, but it was twelve years more before the persevering Prior, although he searched all over England, could find eight oak trees of the dimensions necessary for the mighty angle posts and realise his dream.

But after an hour or two I grew oppressed with the dumbness of all this beauty and wanted to hear its voice. So I called upon the organist, and together we climbed up to the dizzy heights of the triforium and explored the inmost recesses of Harrison's fine new organ, and then, with a really sympathetic generosity rarely shown by cathedral organists to the intruding stranger, he left me for a little to play by myself. Gradually, in whispers first, and long slow waves of sound advancing and retiring, and then as the farthest distances were gradually awakened, in thunders, the whole glorious fabric gave me back its voice. It was not my music, but the music of the cathedral; there is no such ecstatic and artistic collaboration as that which is possible in such an experience, for the building is alive and will answer to you, thrill for you, whisper and tremble for you, if you are patient and have the instinct to find the tonal and rhythmic progressions that are the key to its acoustic secret. When you thus play in such a building, with understanding and without self-consciousness, it is as though the cathedral were singing to itself.

Afterwards I went down under the lantern and listened to the organ while its own master played upon it with excellent skill. I delighted in its many beauties, in the delicate family of viols which are its chief distinction, in the smooth and velvety diapasons, and in the tubas, whose majesty and smoothness of tone might awaken some of the sleeping saints to preparation for the Last Judgment. Lewis's tubas at Southwark seem to me always to be like flames; Willis's at St. Paul's to be like coals of fire that eat their way into the heart of the harmony; Harrison's at Ely suggest, not red heat, but white heat, and seem to reach a point of physical fusion between sound and light at which sound becomes incandescent.

When I came out of the cathedral the mists had cleared away and the sun had come out, and the whole bulk and length and height of the building, like a scarp or mountain in a flat land, filled the horizon and seemed to follow me as I went down the road to the station. There I came back to strange unrealities; the railway bun and sandwich, the grotesque ritual of the railway station, the damp and dusty construction in which I was to be hurried back to London. There is indeed a living soul in all beautiful things, and a corruption as of death in all things ugly, dishonest, and inefficient. Certainly as I came back that morning it was the cathedral that seemed real and living to me, and the things about me which spoke of a dead and dark age of superstitions and abuses. I sat remembering what I had seen and considering the wonder and worth of it. The presbytery at Ely, a presbytery of six bays, with its clustered marble piers, its wealth of floriate capitals, and still richer corbels that hold up the marble shafts of the vault, with all its glory of sculpture and design, cost five thousand pounds— the equivalent, I am told, of about ninety thousand pounds of our money. That is what they did with their money in those days; and to-day there are people who think it a creditable thing to collect a quarter of a million to buy—the Crystal Palace.

Max's Secret

. . . *No collector, I. Not mine the proud anxiety of portfolios of French drawings, or cabinets of Sèvres and Dresden, or great basons and tankards of William and Mary silver, or gems of the Italian Renaissance, or collections of jade, majolica, harpsichords, first editions, ivories, copes, enamels or scarabœi, or any other of the treasures by which men advertise their taste or gratify their vanity. Mine the humbler, pleasanter part of mere critic and appraiser. I am content that my friends should possess and that I should merely enjoy. Bending over their collections with a few well-chosen words of discerning praise, I am credited with unerring judgment and faultless taste. Enough.*

But I stray from the point. I have a sheet of stout white paper before me, a new pen in my hand, and an article of value[1] beside me. Why should I delay to give judgment? I am sitting in my cosy room; a bright fire burns in the hearth, and its crackle mingles pleasantly with the murmur of London without my curtained windows. The hour approaches midnight; no one will disturb me; the telephone bell will not ring; that marble bust, to which annually on Shakespeare's birthday I climb by means of a step ladder and reverently affix a chaplet of laurel,

[1] *A Christmas Garland.* Woven by Max Beerbohm.

*beams down upon me from my bookcase. In nowise
daunted, inspired rather, by that august regard, I
dip my pen in the ink. Glossy black shines, liquid
ebony, on snow-white quill. Yes, reader, I admit it ;
when I write I am fain of a quill. Those curving
bundles, rubber-cinct, feather-tipped, are symbols to
me of the days when I, fond youth, did wander forth
upon the flowery slopes of Parnassus, and slake my
infant thirst at the springs of Helicon. Now, when
everyone carries a black pocket-barrel that empties
itself in a flash, they are rare ornaments of the writer's
table ; and save in the musty recesses of venerable
clubs, and on the fair porphyry of altars furnished
daily by assiduous grooms of chambers, you do nowhere
find them enstacked. I am glad to pay tribute to them
here. Their dull odour, faintly reminiscent of the
goose and therefore repugnant to the nostrils of the
vulgar, is more delicious to me, more melancholy sweet,
than scent of soever long-stored rose-leaves. . . . But
I have wandered into sentiment. Back to the point,
then——*

And the point is, as Mr. Max Beerbohm has
parodied everybody except himself, even though he
has caricatured himself, I contribute this fragment
to be included in some future edition of his *Garland*.

To say that a man has no enemies is, as a rule,
to say that he has no qualities ; a rule to which
Mr. Max Beerbohm is a distinguished exception.
What is his secret ? Is it the pursuit of some safe
and neutral occupation ? Is it merely the habit
of amiability ? Or is it that most common of all
methods of the unhated—the negative method of
never being or doing anything that can command

either hate or love? Clearly the method of Max is not to be found among these. He pursues the most dangerous of trades — that of critic and caricaturist; he is constantly making studies of people's weaker or more grotesque sides; he is an inveterate teller of the truth; and there are no habits so likely as these to earn for their possessor the hatred and ill-will of his fellow-men. Yet no one hates Max; no one bears him ill-will. Why? Why should he thus walk immune when the rest of us suffer in the cause of truth? Why should he be found supping joyfully in the house of the rich Jew whose nasal and other disadvantages he has so ruthlessly exaggerated? Why should the acquaintance whom he has just depicted as a kind of tall candle guttering over its socket weary you with praises of his character and personality? Why, in short, should quite stupid and commonplace people, who are unworthy to speak well of him, and who ought to be incapable of appreciating him, speak of him with both warmth and appreciation? The secret is a double one; it is to be found in his writings and in his drawings. To his personality as a writer intelligent English readers need no introduction; but all of them who are within reach of London would do well, when there is opportunity, to supplement their knowledge of Max by a careful study of the caricature exhibited there, from time to time, and see if they cannot arrive with me at the solution of the mystery which he presents.

Nothing need be said about his technique, which is perfectly simple and direct, and entirely adapted to his particular mode of expression.

It is the human significance of his drawings that
distinguishes them from a host of other caricatures
no less technically competent. It is commonly
said, by people who insist upon reading what they
know of Max's personality into his work, that
good humour is characteristic of all these caricatures. To me that seems nonsense. They are
not in the least good-humoured ; there is none of
that bland, insufferable, patronising kindness of
the caricaturist, who says, " I know you have a
red and bulbous nose, but I will not draw attention
to it ; rather let me depict and exaggerate your
innate goodness of heart." If his subject has a
red and bulbous nose, the wide and childlike vision
of Max will not only observe it, but be fascinated
by it until it fills the foreground of his picture.
He is no more good-natured than he is ill-natured ;
his vision, as I have said, is as frank and curious
as that of a child who, seated in an omnibus, fixes
his embarrassing gaze on anything at all odd or
unfortunate in the appearance of the person
opposite to him. Thus no one who comes into his
field of vision escapes. The body of Mr. Sargent
swells, and his head dwindles, like the body and head
of a man seen in a bilious nightmare. Lord
Rosebery's pale, round eyes grow rounder and paler
and blanker. The chorus-girl prettiness of the
Rev. R. J. Campbell, the heavy, bovine patience
and rumination of Mr. W. L. Courtney, the hollow
and pretentious domination of Mr. Alfred de
Rothschild, the busybody importance of Sir Sidney
Colvin, and the compact and sinister power of
the late Sir George Lewis, come inevitably into

the front of the pictures, characteristics from which, like the child in the omnibus, we cannot remove our eyes. Only rarely does the observation seem to fail, as, for example, in the case of Count Benckendorff, who in Max's eyes is surely less of a *grand seigneur* than he appears in actual life ; or in the case of the Duke of Marlborough, whose personality in Max's drawing has an importance which it is far from possessing in the flesh. The rest of the caricatures have all the fidelity which one meets with only in good portraiture ; that is to say, you would not recognise a face from your knowledge of one of these caricatures, but you recognise the drawing instantly for its likeness to the face you know, and, studying it, you seem to add to your knowledge of the original personality.

I observed that soon after the opening of these exhibitions a large proportion of the drawings are marked as sold ; and I cannot help wondering who it is that buys them, and from what motives. For these are emphatically not caricatures of the kind that the victim always likes to hang upon his study wall. They are the kind which the enemy of the victim would like to hang upon *his* study wall. Were they bought, then, by enemies of the people portrayed ? Probably not, for it is a rare and respectable enmity that would spend five-and-twenty pounds on the privilege of gloating over the distorted features of the hated one. No, I think the subjects themselves are the buyers ; and I think they buy these caricatures so that their enemies may not be able to possess them, and they probably hang them in a dark passage or pretend they have lost them. Or else, being compelled to exhibit them, they say with an indulgent smile, " Yes, that is a drawing Max did of me ; not one of his best, I think." But they have bought them and paid for them, and the amiable and gentle Max takes his toll of them and, if he had an enemy, might thus be represented as adding to his other dangerous trades that of levying a kind of artistic blackmail. And yet he walks through life smiled upon by everybody. The mystery deepens.

The careful observer will note among the portraits of people adorning the walls of this exhibition a considerable proportion of the climbing fraternity ; Sir Gilbert Parker is indeed wonderfully depicted in the very act of climbing a ladder ; but he is only one among many of the great social band whose feet we hear upon the stairs and whose motto is " Excelsior." Upon these Max seems to lavish his art with the greatest affection, so that London is full of people who are going about half in hope and half in fear that he will make caricatures of them. In hope, because to be caricatured by Max is a definite stage in climbing ; to a man in politics or art it is what being painted by Sargent is to a woman in Society ; and in biographies of these people we read either, " Presented in 1890 ; painted by Sargent in 1896 " ; or " Entered Parliament in 1890 ; caricatured by Max Beerbohm 1896." In fear, because one never knows what dread secret, which we had thought was known only to ourselves and our mirror, the childlike pen of Max will not reveal. He is thus at once the scourge and the reward of the climbers; the pleasant scourge, the bitter reward. But as Balzac has truly said, "Parvenus are like monkeys; seen from above, we admire their agility in climbing, but when they have reached the top it is only their more shameful parts that are visible."

Some of his caricatures are extremely severe, such as the group of well-known Jews, favourites of the late Court, entitled, "Are we as welcome as ever?": some are notably sympathetic, like those of Mr. George Moore, whose melancholy sensitiveness broods always over the dull, cold eye of the realist; and that of Sir George Frampton, who merely seems, as he seems in the flesh, always to be about to face rough weather. And some are extremely funny, notably those of Dawn meeting Mr. Robert Hichens in the Desert, the Archbishop of Canterbury in his seat in the House of Lords, and Sir Alfred Mond congratulating Mr. Austin Harrison on the current issue of the *English Review*. Most of them are severely true; but there is one person upon whom Max is never severe, and that is himself. His eyelashes may curl a little more, and his forehead bulge a little more, but his eyelashes and his forehead are things upon which Max need not fear to dwell. He is entirely indulgent to himself, and herein he exhibits his true sincerity; for if we do not appreciate our own good points, who else is likely to?

Both as a writer and a draughtsman Max has most curiously earned a reputation as a kind of fantastic person, some one who is never serious, who is always playing and posing. That is a very stupid and unintelligent misconception. His most striking quality, and the real secret of that immunity with which he practises dangerous arts, is his sincerity. There are two ways, remember, of telling the truth; you may tell it sincerely, and you may tell it insincerely. Now the truth is such a dangerous thing that it cannot safely be handled with affectation or insincerity. If you decide to tell the truth you must not only be in earnest about telling it, but, in writing at any rate, you must learn and practise how to do it. Sincerity is not a natural gift; it is a fine art. Hardly anyone can be naturally sincere. Long before he learns to be natural, the child has begun to learn to veil and disguise his natural impulses. Even the dog and the cat practise a lifelong dissimulation, and their lapses into sincerity are apt to be treated as startling misdemeanours. But the artist has to learn to be sincere and natural; to discover, by bold facing of facts and clear and honest reflection, what he really thinks or feels; and then he must learn and labour to say it in the simplest possible language. All this Max has done in his writings and in his drawings. Do not for a moment regard either as airy trifles; rightly considered they are serious and formidable, and in the case of personal studies all the more serious and formidable if the subjects of them imagine them to be conceived in the spirit of good-humoured banter.

Like many people who build on the solid rock, Max has chosen to surround his work with a ring of laughter. The dull and ignorant, approaching it in the dark, are aware only of the ripples on the surface, and think that there is nothing beyond ; but across the moat, and protected by it from the desecrating feet of fools, is a castle that lifts its towers to the clear sky.

Rosemary and Baubles

I WAS looking the other day in the British Museum at some of the toys with which little children played in Egypt thousands of years ago, and also at some of those which in a later age enlivened the nurseries of Greece and Rome. And afterwards, wandering through the bewildering galleries of a modern Christmas toy fair, I could not but be struck, not only by the essentially changeless nature of our playthings, but also by the tendency manifested throughout the ages for toys to become over-elaborate and complicated until, like civilisation itself, they defeat their own ends and have to revert to elementary simplicity again. The little Egyptian children had simple things like soft balls or hard ones made of porcelain or papyrus, and the most elaborate toys of theirs which I have seen are two quite simple little figures, one a bronze woman carrying a vessel on her head, and the other, in earthenware, a mother carrying her child. But the little Romans and Greeks were much more complicated in their tastes, and there are still in existence dolls of theirs elaborately dressed, with jointed arms and legs, and tiny doll's-houses chairs and tables, with little cups and utensils of pottery painted with scenes from the lives of children.

In our own age there have been many developments of elaborateness in toys, which perhaps were brought to their perfection in the workshops of South Germany in the sixteenth and seventeenth centuries ; and we are just now at the culmination of another similar, although less noble development, and on the eve of a return, apparently, to simpler and more primitive toys. Certainly although the childish ambition is to have something which " works " and is " real," it is not these things which abide most securely in our memories and affections ; but things which were so unreal as to be mere grotesque symbols of what they were supposed to represent. In fact it was the toys which gave us most to do, and laid on our imaginations the greatest task of pretence and make-believe, that really won our hearts. How simple are the first things with which a little child learns to play ! First something soft that can be taken into the mouth ; then something that rattles or jingles ; then the simple ball or sphere that can be rolled or bounced, then the doll in some shape or form ; then the wheel, and then according to the child's inclination or opportunity, the reins that help him to pretend to be a horse, the sword or helmet which makes him into a soldier, the gun for killing enemies or wild beasts, the railway train, the boat, and so on. The most precious toys which I remember were an imperfectly cured cowhorn which gave out, in addition to its wavering note, a most overpowering smell ; a species of gaily painted wheel mounted on a handle, which I called (quite inaccurately) my

" whirligig " ; a small boat with black topsides and a salmon-coloured bottom, which has sailed many voyages on the green tablecloth, now bringing up alongside Webster's Dictionary to discharge cargo, and now lying at anchor in the shelter of a promontory of Bibles ; and a common iron hoop burnished by friction of its stick to the colour of silver, beside and behind which I ran, over paved footpaths dappled with sunshine filtered through the hawthorn and laburnum of suburban gardens, many a long, unweary mile. It is strange to me to think that these objects, once so living and crowded upon with poetry and imagination, so closely associated with all that was lovely and adventurous in the mind of childhood, must long ago have crumbled away and been restored to their chemical elements, and that I should still be walking about and looking into toyshop windows, reduced to the sorry business of writing about toys instead of gloriously playing with them. But it is of no use. I made an experiment not very long ago ; did actually purchase for an absurdly small sum, a clock-work railway of a kind that was totally beyond my reach in the days when I would have gloried in it ; and carrying it home in a large red cardboard box, and making sure that my servant was well out of the way, did actually set it out on the floor and attempt to play with it. But the glory had departed ; I could not become sufficiently like a little child to enter into that kingdom. But I knew what to do with the train. I parcelled it up again and bestowed it upon a family of little children into whose wildest dreams the idea of possessing such a thing could never have entered, and I believe it is to this day brought out on a Sunday or a birthday by their father, and played with for their benefit, surrounded in their minds with the same glamour and glory in which it first fell upon them from the skies.

I am constantly seeing my little friends being deprived of this great pleasure of the rarely used " best " toy. Everything is delivered into their hands—aeroplanes that fly, electric trains with signals and switches that work, toy battleships and motor-cars that are marvels of ingenuity, armies that are patterns of accuracy in their uniforms and equipment. But when you have put into a child's hand an extremely elaborate model, it cannot and does not satisfy his imagination. He will play for a whole day with a train made of chairs, because imagination enters into the game ; the arm-chair is an engine, the sofa is a sleeping-car, another arm-chair is the luggage-van. But if you give him a perfect thing his imagination is left out in the cold ; there is no part for it to take in the game except a destructive part ; in short, there is nothing to be done with the mechanical model except to break it open and see how it works. Indeed, more summary methods are quite natura-ally attractive. I have seen a little boy of four years old, to whom an elaborate working model of a motor-car had been presented, after watching it work for a few minutes, take it up in his hand and hurl it to the ground with a smile of satisfaction. It was the only thing he could think of doing with it. That is why the hoop or the train of chairs or

the rough and grotesque toy train will always give
more real pleasure than the most elaborate machinery that can be conceived; that is why the rag
doll or the woolly lamb will always lie nearer the
heart's affections than the most wonderfully
equipped and elaborately clothed French *poupée*.

As I have said, however, I believe there is some
sign of a return to the more primitive style of toy.
I see mysterious objects in toyland with quaint
names, of which the golliwog and the teddy bear
were the precursors. There is one which particularly pleases me called " A dada." I like it first
for its name; it is not called " dada " or " the
dada," but " a dada "; and it has thus been
christened, I suppose, in order to faciliate reference
to it by the very youngest of its possessors.
It is, moreover, a simple doll, of a bright and
cheery countenance, and can be made by simple
means to assume various postures. It is more
natural and purely primitive than the rather
affected and artificial type of American invention
known as " Billykins "; in fact, it is a charming
and attractive toy, which will probably take an
abiding place among those " solid joys and lasting
pleasures " which happy children should be laying
up for themselves in the fragrant cabinet of
memory. A touch of the grotesque is admirable
in a toy; it separates it from the common things
of life, and gives definition to the memories associated with it; but it should above all things
be simple. Do you remember those trains stamped
out of tin, with wheels of brass wire, and no resemblance at all to any known vehicle? Was there

ever a red like that of the red carriage, or a yellow and a blue like the colours that followed it; or any green to equal the greenness of the engine? Do you remember the fragrant smell of them— yes, and the taste of them when licked? Or do you remember a little *passe-partout* glass box edged with yellow, containing a tortoise that trembled and shook whenever the box was moved? When the mind is putting out its first feelers towards beauty, it is things like this vivid, definite, and comprehensible, which enchant and satisfy it, yet lead it on to the pursuit of ever finer things. Pray think of this when you are making the choice, so wearisome to you, so momentous to them, of Christmas toys for your little friends.

.   .   .   .   .   .

When people grow up and become possessed of the numerous and elaborate toys for which their ambition has striven, a curious change takes place in their attitude towards those who come to play with them. In the nursery the sentiment inspired by the possession of toys is, as a rule, simply selfish. The child desires to enjoy them alone, to exercise his own imagination upon them; and he is apt to look askance at visiting playmates, and to resent the suggestion that they should be allowed to play with the particular toys which are highest in his favour at the moment. But that attitude departs with experience. The most absorbed man soon finds that the amount of pleasure he can by himself extract from any particular possession is limited. If he be of a kind and generous disposition he wishes to share his pleasures; but even if he be selfish he will desire that others shall see him using his toys. In all sports that are enjoyed in association, such as hunting and shooting, this principle is active, although it is entirely subconscious. In addition to enjoying a day's hunting people like to show off their horses, or to have witnesses of their extraordinary and continuous propinquity to hounds. And in addition to the joy of hitting a difficult mark and all the other pleasures of the covert side, there is for the man who shoots well a certain sober joy in having other people to see it and know it. Thus it happens that the man who is possessed of toys constantly invites others who are less fortunate to share his pleasures. And it is in the interest of those who themselves are without luxurious possessions, and who are continually invited to partake of the hospitality of people who have, that I would offer a few words of advice concerning the use of other people's toys.

It not infrequently happens that the man without possessions knows a good deal more about their use than the proud proprietor. Not always, of course, but often. If that be your case, my poor friend, be careful to conceal your knowledge. There was a time, perhaps, when you had motor-cars and your friend had not; and out of your large experience perhaps you taught him what little he knows about them, and started him on his career as a possessor of them. And here comes a curious instance of the influence of property. If you still possess a motor-car your pupil will, in matters connected with his own, still treat you possibly with deference, and at the least as an equal. But if you should cease, and he continue, to possess, even although your experience increases too, a change will come over his attitude towards you. He will become ever so slightly patronising, and if you differ from him or venture to point out anything in which you think him mistaken, he will immediately take refuge in the fact of possession. He will even explain to you that his car is in some mysterious way different from others of the same class; but really the only difference is that he possesses it, that it belongs to him, that he has paid for it, and that even though his ideas about it be wrong he can afford to act as though they were right. My advice to you in these circumstances is not to argue with him; to accept the nonsense he talks and let him suppose that you agree with him. Perhaps you are driving his car; you may be an expert and he a blundering, gear-chipping beginner; but when he nervously asks, on your approaching a piece of country such as you have driven through thousands of times, "Would you like me to take her here, as it's a bad bit of road and I know the car?" surrender your place with alacrity. Try not to be irritated or alarmed at the series of mistakes which he proceeds to commit; he really thinks that this particular car is safer in his hands than in yours, although he might admit that any other car would be safer in yours than in his. It belongs to him, you see, it is the only car he knows, and he not unnaturally thinks that its qualities are as peculiar to it as they are unique in his own experience.

There is perhaps a certain rough justice in all this, because it often happens that the man who spends the first part of his life making himself expert in the appreciation of luxuries must spend the second part of his life in going without them. The man who has them is the man who was doing something else while you were studying them. He may be a boor and a duffer in his use of them, but he has got them, and you must remember that all your knowledge and experience in their use will be lightly esteemed by him unless you have got them too. It is a nice point for you to consider whether you would rather be cultivated in the knowledge of beautiful or luxurious or amusing things without possessing them, or possess them without knowledge. The combination of both states is rare. How many men who possess a fine cellar of wine have a real palate, or could tell the difference between a Corton and a Romanée? And how many men who have a really discriminating palate possess a cellar of wine? If you have known what it is in youth, when according to copy-book rules you should have been saving money, to spend your whole available capital upon a meal and a bottle of old wine, you are not likely to be rich in your old age. Not rich in money I mean; you may be rich in knowledge, and must comfort yourself with the reflection that possession does not imply either knowledge or understanding of the things possessed. It is really better, if you have the strength of mind, to abstain altogether from playing with other people's toys, and merely to look on at their attempts to enjoy themselves, and applaud. But it is not everyone who can resist the temptation to enjoy the good things which are offered to him. So if you ride your friend's horse be prepared to learn afterwards, if he commits any fault, that he is a very discriminating animal who knows very well when anyone is on his back with whom he can take liberties. If your friend sails his yacht within a bowsprit's length of someone else's main boom, it is a tricky and expert piece of steering ; but remember that if you do it you will be held to have had a narrow and fortuitous escape from disaster. If he takes a long shot in his own deer-forest and misses, well, it was a justifiable risk ; if you do so it was an impossible shot which ought not to have been attempted. Do not suppose for a moment, when your friend hideously vamps upon his new Steinway grand, that what he wants is to hear its tone brought out, and that he would enjoy it more if you, with most exquisite artistic finish, should perform an impromptu of Chopin. He would be merely in a state of fidgets and ill-concealed impatience until you had finished, when he would make haste to take your place as one who should say, " Now let us hear the real tone." He does not want to hear beautiful tone ; he wants to play upon his own piano, and to hear with his own ears the noises which he makes with his own fingers.

Apparently, from all this, the man who understands things without possessing them comes off much worse than the man who possesses them without understanding ; the one has all the suffering and the other all the fun. The only consolation for the non-possessor lies in the knowledge that if his friend has the accident of possession, he has the certainty of knowledge ; and there are many things which it is better to understand than to possess. The ideal thing is to do both ; although sometimes I think it is only the things which we understand that we can be said to possess, and that the only things which we can really understand are the things which we truly love.

The Neglect of Wine

I SUPPOSE there is more wine bought in
England about Christmas-time than at any
other; and at no season are there so many
outrages committed upon the spirit of the vine.
Tepid Champagne, warm Burgundy, icy young
Bordeaux (uncorked the moment before it is served)
and crusty Port decanted within a day or two of its
arrival by railway, are regular incidents of the
festive season. Yet inasmuch as the liquid so
treated is often drunk more as a symbol of festivity
than for any love of its intrinsic qualities, it may be
said to serve at least one of its purposes—which is,
even by such strange misuses, to make glad the
heart of man.

But it is not the people whose annual outbreak
of headaches they never dream of associating
with the unwonted mixture of fearsome vintages
that I accuse of neglect of wine, but rather the
possessors of cellars and the people who drink
it daily and habitually. The ignorance about wine
in England, even among those who have every
opportunity of studying it, is colossal. The English
butler, to whose grim mercies the whole matter
is too often left, is an arch offender in this
respect; the wine-merchant is sometimes another,
and the family doctor is a third. To the majority

of physicians wine is simply wine, a medium for the administration of alcohol in mild doses. The difference in medicinal values between, let us say, a Château Margaux 1890 and a Romanée or Chambertin of 1904, is a mystery to them; although the alternative and curative properties of the Bordeaux and the toning and vitalising effects of the Burgundy are so different as to be almost opposite in their physiological effects. And I may add that there is not one household in a thousand in England where a bottle of either of these vintages could be brought to the table from the cellar in its proper condition for drinking. The butler (and indeed the owner of the wine) would see to that.

The wholesale murder of rare wine goes on daily in England; a veritable massacre of the innocents. There are thousands of dozens of rare vintage wines in English cellars which have either perished long since or are gradually perishing from neglect and improper treatment. " I know you like Burgundy," said a friend to me the other day; " I have some wonderful old stuff in the cellar; I don't know what it is, but I know it's very, very old. I ordered up a bottle for you." I feared the worst and waited. In five minutes I heard the loud pop of a cork, and the butler appeared, jauntily carrying—oh, horror! a decanter. To decant a very old Burgundy in that manner would of itself be enough to ruin it, and there was further evidence that the decanter had actually been warmed. Of course the wine was absolutely dead, and tasted of nothing at all but weak vinegar. Another bottle was brought up and, at my earnest request, carried carefully to the table in its cradle, and the cork gently and carefully drawn as it lay there. There was just the suggestion of a ghost of a wine—nothing more. It turned out to be an old Corton which twenty years ago must have been in its glory; but which, kept in the same cellar as Bordeaux, and exposed to frequent changes of temperature, had probably suffered great deterioration of character before it had died ten years ago of old age. There was nothing to be done with the whole bin but pour it away, although if I had suggested this, my friend would have regarded me as a very ignorant fellow, for he was one of those who cannot believe that a famous vintage wine which had lain for over half a century undisturbed in the dust of his cellars could be anything but precious, and the more precious the older it grew. In the same cellar were thousands of bottles of the wines of Champagne, Bordeaux, of the Rhine, the Mosel, and the Saar—yes, and even of Oporto—all suffering a similar fate; things that had once been mighty and glorious now fallen to decay or death; while their owner was drinking undistinguished wine from the Stores, ordered month by month, in order to " save " the contents of the cellar. And this is only an example of what is going on in hundreds of houses in England where the wine cellars, instead of being shrines in which the fruit of the most perfect marriages between sun and soil is resting and growing and developing a mature and generous vitality, are mere catacombs or mausoleums containing the corpses and envelopes of what were once living things, but from which the life principle—and with it all their use and beauty and beneficence for us—has long since fled.

For it is also a fact of which people are surprisingly ignorant that wine has a life of its own ; that in every bottle there is actually some germ or principle which curiously corresponds with the animating principle within ourselves. Like us, it knows youth and age and death ; like us, it knows sickness and health ; like us, it is liable to destruction either from disease within itself or from shock or accident from without. Like the life of men, it has the inimitable charm of youth, and " awkward age " of development, a strength of maturity, an increasing mellowness and sunset decline of age. It passes through certain changes of life, and is sensitive, like all living things, to the changes of the earthly seasons. Deep down in the chalk of the Burgundy district, far from any effect of heat or cold, where the mercury in the thermometer never moves from one year's end to the other, sealed and corked hermetically from the atmosphere, the wine is nevertheless reached by those same subtle forces that move and stir in our blood at the vernal and autumnal equinoxes. At such times a bottle of wine will become sick and deranged, and in a week or two will become well and sound again. Like our three score and ten, there is appointed for every bottle of healthy wine a span of life which varies considerably according to the amount of sunshine in the year of its birth, and according to the state of the soil and the plants. A bottle of Champagne of a good vintage may last as long as twenty years; a rare Port that has been bottled two instead of three years after the vintage may last for seventy; and other wines in proportion, according to their vinosity. There are exceptions, of course. Just before the war I tasted, from a magnum of Perrier Jouet 1876, wine that could still foam a little in the glass and whose flavour remained delicate and characteristic, although its strength was far gone; and the fellow to this magnum had actually blown out its cork as it lay in the bin during the hot summer of 1911. Such valiancy, such vigour of old age, are rare indeed in the wines of Champagne, which, if they come of a good vintage, are at their best between the tenth and fifteenth years of their age.

But our neglect of wine in England is shown in many other ways than by the mere ignorance of elementary facts concerning it. The increased consumption of Champagne has done much to oust other wines from favour. Champagne is pre-eminently the drink of social London; it goes best, perhaps, with the hurried feverish life that we lead. But a curious thing about the drinking of Champagne is that, apart from being a taste, it becomes a habit, like drug-taking or cigarette smoking; and this adds formidably to the effect of its rivalry with other wines. It is all very well to drink Champagne if you drink only the best; yet there are thousands of people who habitually spend on a bottle of indifferent Champagne a sum which would procure them a Bordeaux or

Burgundy, a Berncastler or Rudesheimer of the
finest vintage. Again, English people have lately
taken to the bad habit of neglecting vintage
Ports for so-called tawny Ports, and innocently
believe that lightness of colour in the wine
is a measure of its harmlessness; whereas many
of these wines from the wood are crude liquor,
doctored for the wine-merchant's trade; taste of
sugar instead of wine, and burn on the throat
like young Cognac. True tawny Port should
be as dry as sand, unsweetened and unforti-
fied; otherwise the true Port flavour is found
only in vintage wines which have matured in the
bottle.

But why should Port be our only after-dinner
wine? How foolish it is of people whose means
enable them to have the best of such things that
the world affords to confine themselves to the
banal round of Hock or Sauterne for luncheon,
and Champagne and Port for dinner! Lovely,
delicate Burgundies, the sun-filled Château wines
of Bordeaux, the gorgeous and recuperative and
truly imperial Tokay, the old Amontillados and
Olorosos of Spain, the Boals and Malmseys of
Madeira, to say nothing of the rarer wines of
Hungary and Austria (but not of Italy)—here in
essence are the sunshine and soil of a thousand happy
slopes where the very essences of life are steeped
and concentrated. It seems a pity to neglect
them; and one of these days some physician will
make a fortune who, instead of studying fashionable
drugs, which in his heart he despises, turns his
attention to the curative and hygienic properties

of different wines ; who orders his happy patients
perhaps a goblet of Château d'Yquem, or, perad-
venture, a couple of glasses of old Tokay—one
when the sun is at the meridian, and one when he
is at his setting.

Who's Who?

WHO, indeed? I have been searching through the two thousand odd pages of the new edition of the famous red book, in order to find out. I have been trying to discover what exactly it is, what quality, or combination of qualities, that entitle one to the relative pronoun. It is not fame, for I have looked in vain for particulars of the lives and careers of some eminent music-hall artists, who are probably among the most famous people in England, people about whose lives I would gladly learn some particulars; but I find not even the name of Harry Lauder.* So it is not fame. It is not character and attainment; for some of the men of the highest character and of the most consummate attainment who are known to me find no place in the pages of this book. It is not merely great official position, or aristocratic birth, for thousands of these biographies are concerned with people who have no official position, and are of what is called obscure origin. What is it, then? As far as I can make out, the people whose names you will find in these pages are for the most part people who either have been born with, or in their course through life have acquired, a

* This was written before Sir Harry received the honour of knighthood.

label of some kind with which to distinguish their personality. They are the people concerning whom the question, What is he? can be readily and plainly answered. And in this respect the book really reflects admirably the condition of our complex and well-mixed society. To the small world of Society there is, for a man at any rate, only really one rule of admission. He must be, not someone, but something, that people can easily remember. This is contrary to the common and fond superstition that membership of the very mixed club of Metropolitan society implies all kinds of qualifications. It does not. All that is necessary is that a man should speak the language and have the habits of that society; that he should know and be known to a considerable number of other members; and above all, that he should possess some label by which he can be identified, and by which he can be rapidly described when the inevitable question is asked, "Who is that man who sat opposite to me at dinner?" His name may be plain Mr. Abel Cain; that may convey nothing at all; but when the pendant description is added, "You know—the controller of this, the editor of that, the man who runs the other thing, the writer, the owner, inventor, organiser, believer in, fugitive from, desirer of, partner with, settler on, speculator in, so and so," he takes his place in the ordered world and becomes entitled to a paragraph in *Who's Who*. The title of the book should rather be either *Who's What* or *What's Who*; for the question "Who's Who?" is really never answered.

It is not a little strange that a man should thus

be identified by qualities, occupations, or achievements, which he shares with numberless other people, rather than by his own individuality, which he shares with no one. If a name could only be put so that it would be the true distinction and identification. There are thousands of peers, painters, writers, soldiers, baronets, professors, heads of this, that, and the other. In what a man does he can never be original. But the miracle of individuality remains, and personality, as far as we know, is never duplicated, never repeated throughout infinite time. My copy of *Who's Who* opens easily and naturally at that page on which my own name appears. No one knows better than I how futile is this paragraph in attempting to answer the question, Who I am. I see there a list of statements of fact in which the best face and most imposing presentment possible are made of my small record of doings. It grows a little longer year by year, and will soon disappear from these pages, to be replaced by a line in the obituary list, and thereafter as a record vanish utterly from the mind of man. Concerning what I do and have done, I say, there is certain rather unnecessary information here ; of what I am and have been, no information at all. So that, to return to our friend Mr. Abel Cain, it is no answer to the question, " Who's who ? " as applied to him to say " C. M. G. 1908 ; Commissioner for Oaths in the Cockahoopoo Islands 1909 ; Assistant Commissioner 1907 ; Deputy Assistant Commissioner 1903 ; born, etc., etc., etc., etc." The nearest answer to the question would be contained in the

entry, " Cain, Adam Abel, C.M.G. ; Adam Abel
Cain." And even that would be only a label too,
for our very names are not private or peculiar to
us ; they are worn by other people in our own
and other times, whose lives and individualities
are as distant from our own as that of his Highness
Maharana Shri Mohandevji Narandevji, Maharana
of Dharampur, is different from the Reverend
John Jones, author of *Elims of Life.*

Having regard to the great and increasing bulk
of this book, one cannot help thinking that the
time has come when some revision of the system
on which it is edited should be attempted. It is
already in price beyond the means of many, even
of the people whose names are to be found in it ;
and the addition of a vast number of biographies
of eminent foreigners, while adding to its use as a
work of reference, has increased its size to the
point of unwieldiness. It is a pity, I think, that
the length at which a person's achievements, and
the achievements of his ancestors, and his recreations should be set forth, should depend entirely
upon his own sense of proportion. An even superficial study of these pages convinces me that that
sense is not a safe guide. I have before me a
notice nearly a page long devoted to the biography
of a painter and journalist whose name I had
not heard before. It sets forth immediately after
his name that he is a member of the Society of
Authors ; and, as anybody can be that for a guinea,
it is not worth a line in *Who's Who.* It tells us
that his father was a landowner, and that he
adopted his present name by Deed Poll, 1894.

It tells us what profession he was intended for, although he did not pursue it ; it tells us the schools at which he studied, and the names of the masters ; where he painted and exhibited pictures ; and sets forth at great length the titles of articles which he contributed to various sixpenny magazines, with the names of the magazines. It seems to me that some mild editorial curb should be applied to enthusiasm of this kind. And as for people's recreations, information about them may give the reader some cynical amusement if he have the patience to study them, but they are rather silly, and mostly untrue. I mean that the majority of people who describe their recreations as shooting, hunting, fishing, polo, and so forth, are people to whom these are not recreations, but hard work ; whose real recreation, did they but know it, is a little serious reading or labour. Attempts at facetiousness under the heading of recreations are generally failures. The Reverend Silvester Horne's " golfing, cycling, and agitation " is a fair example ; also the Reverend Prebendary Carlile's " open-air preaching " and Colonel Maude's " Nil." Sometimes they are pathetic, as in the entry " formerly polo, hunting, steeplechasing, deer-stalking, shooting ; now golf, walking, reading." There are about twenty-five thousand biographies; I think the word golf occurs nearly twenty thousand times. There is one man who gives his recreation as bulb-growing. It seems to be a somewhat periodic and intermittent thing to be dependent upon for one's recreation. It is exciting enough, to be sure, when the bulbs are coming up, and interesting enough when the ground is being prepared, but I imagine that there must be long days in the summer and autumn which must hang rather heavy on the hands of this contributor.

For the point of entertainment this book would be considerably enlivened by a reduction of the number of biographies of military officers who are possessed of inferior decorations. There might be something to be said for printing biographies of all officers of the rank of captain and over who have not received the D.S.O., and of all the colonial officials who have escaped the C.M.G. That would reduce the size of the book by about a quarter; and if the distinguished foreigners were relegated to a separate volume, it might be possible to reduce the book to something like its former size and price of five shillings. For my part, I felt some five-and-twenty years ago, when my own name was first included, that the book had then reached an ideal stage of convenience and completeness, and that the addition of further names was unnecessary. But I suppose there are other people who have been arriving at that opinion every year since then.

The Fashion is Always Beautiful

THE other day I heard a group of women at luncheon discussing, with the charming gravity which they always bring to bear on matters of personal adornment, the fashions of the immediate future. One of them had just returned, from a shopping expedition to Paris, and the others listened to her reports much as the headquarter staff in a great campaign might listen to news brought in by scouts and patrols, on whose depositions their information must be based. This lady electrified the others by assuring them that they would all be wearing flounces next year. Everything, she said, was going in the direction of flounces ; whereupon two of her audience expressed disappointment and protest, but the third and prettiest said, " But the fashion is always beautiful." For some reason this not very striking expression remained in my memory and haunted me as I went about my affairs ; and as the only way to get rid of such an idea is to think it out, I set myself, when I got home, to consider what amount of truth might lie in it.

If you pass in review through your mind all the fashions in dress which you have known in your own time, you will I think find none that seems so beautiful as that of the present moment.

The Fashion is Always Beautiful

By dress I mean, of course, women's dress and adornment generally, because that is the highest and most artistic form which dress takes with us. I do not mean the extreme of the fashion, or that exaggerated style which likes to overstep the mode a little in every direction; but rather the style of dress worn by pretty women whose clothes are perhaps their chief preoccupation, and who have ample means to cultivate and give expression to their own individual taste as applied to the mode of the moment. It is always, then, the latest fashion which has seemed to us most beautiful. If one leaves out the fashion of the last year or two and reviews those that succeeded them one may, it is true, make critical discrimination among them. Thus the early Victorian fashions were obviously much prettier than the late Victorian, which were, indeed, probably the ugliest that human beings have ever devised. Yet at the time one thought them beautiful—at any rate I know that I did; although now when I turn over those old volumes of *Punch* which were my chief source of information upon social matters I wonder how we could have borne to see our friends so disguised and bedecked.

My earliest studies in clothes and the fashion were made in church—that being the place where I had most material before me to consider and most time in which to consider it. It was the era of bustles, and one watched the people coming down the aisle of the church, each woman carrying on her back a draped protuberance, by the extent, adornment, or " set " of which, among other things, the extent of her adherence to the fashion might be judged. One by one the bustles came in, glided down the aisle, and disappeared into pews. Whether they were sat upon or merely leaned against I had not then, and have not to this day, ascertained; but I have seen them put on, and, in that careless intimacy with which a very small child is made free of the most sacred scenes of feminine toilet, observed a beautiful woman, half clothed, tying by means of a tape a kind of pack or hump stuffed with horsehair upon her back. I remember even at the time thinking it a singularly brutal and undignified scene, like the harnessing of a cart-horse; and the memory and impression remained with me, and often, when almost intoxicated by the dignity with which some bustle or other went rocking down the aisle, I have remembered and visualised the sordid foundation on which it rested, and my joy in it has departed like the joy of one who sees through to the mean motives that lie behind magnificent actions.

Sometimes, if I remember aright, there was substituted for the bustle a kind of cage made of metal girders covered with cloth, although whether this belonged to the bustle era or was some relic of the fashion which had preceded it I do not know. But I remember the mode called the " waterfall," which seemed to me at the time one of the most ravishing things conceivable for the adornment of feminine beauty. The " waterfall " was a group of closely parallel vertical pleats (if that be the proper word), which began somewhere in the small of the back, curved magnificently over the bustle, and descended to the ground. The idea was apparently of a stream of water which, rising somewhere between the shoulder-blades, broke as it were upon the bustle, and poured in a Niagara of pleats to the hem of the garment—comparable, had it only been employed in front instead of the back of the dress, to that river of precious ointment that ran down Aaron's beard to the skirts of his garments. But whatever its origin may have been, there was a day when this device was the very latest fashion; and on that day I for one thought it extremely beautiful.

To take another extreme case of the same kind, I remember a device by which the sleeves, where they joined the shoulders of the dress, sprouted or were continued upwards, giving the impression of either a morbid growth or of shoulders hideously shrugged. These were called "ears"; at first they were flat, like a bat's or mouse's; but, gradually becoming fuller, and the fullness extending further and further down the sleeves, they developed at last into the puffed and swollen sleeves which were the joy of a later day. But there was a day when nobody without ears to her sleeves could be regarded as being properly dressed at all; the absence of them gave a wretchedly poor and mean appearance to the whole person; while the set of a pair of smart ears would of itself be enough to give distinction and chic to their wearer.

It was thus with hair-dressing, with jewellery, and with every kind of garment. You, good reader, may have had all the beauty and romance of your life associated with a being upon whose forehead was reared an edifice of tightly and artificially curled hair; from whose ears depended lumps of gold shaped like a coil of rope, round whose neck hung a locket or kind of safe deposit structure of the same precious metal, and on whose gentle breast there rose and fell a great brooch consisting of a large oval pane of glass behind which, a grisly relic, was stored a mass of human hair; who daily tied upon herself with tapes the stuffy burden of a bustle; whose sleeves sprouted into a pair of ears, and who wore a bonnet and a dolman upon which yards of jet beads and bugles were strung. I remember distinctly—and this has a particularly interesting bearing on my subject —that in my earliest childhood the picture called into my mind by the word " pretty " (and all words are associated in our minds with some picture) was that of a tightly curled fringe. For a long time I thought that to be pretty was to have a fringe; that those who had it could properly be called pretty, and those who lacked it could not. To-day we consider all these things ugly and disfiguring, and we are right; but in their own day we thought them beautiful—they symbolised beauty for us. And although in my own mind I feel convinced that the fashions of to-day are more beautiful than anything in the last two hundred years, at any rate, it is probable that they too, with all their simplicity and fidelity to the beauties of the body's own form, will be regarded by some future generation as—not ugly, perhaps, but at any rate absurd. The real reason, I think, why the fashion is always beautiful, at any rate, while it lasts, is that it is associated with some of the most beautiful things and the most beautiful people that we know ; that it enshrines something more than can appeal merely to the eye—something that springs from the heart, belongs to our griefs and our joys, and is a part of our living and breathing existence. The fashion is a symbol of the contemporary, of the present hour, of life itself ; and as life is always beautiful, it is perhaps for that reason that we are right in finding the fashion beautiful also.

On Missing a Train

THERE are certain accidents in life which, although they cause annoyance at the time, are a means of procuring for us experiences outside our original programme which often turn out to be of advantage to us, and which have the value of all things that are bestowed on us unexpectedly and that seem like additions to our reasonable share of good fortune. Everyone can remember in his or her own experience some such apparent disaster, of a greater or less degree; it may have been an illness, or a disappointment, or a loss, about which we are able to say afterwards, " But for that accident I should never have known So-and-so, or done or possessed such-and-such a thing." The secret of what is called a philosophical mind lies in the conscious realisation of this fact; in the belief that life consists for most of us in an average of fortunate or unfortunate experience, and that the things which seem at first sight most fortunate are apt to turn into something very different, while apparent disaster is generally compensated by some corresponding or resultant advantage. The fact is a commonplace of copy-book moralities. It is the realising it, and the belief that it will really work in our own lives, which is rare enough to make those who possess it seem to be endowed with an extra degree of wisdom and intelligence.

No one, not even the professed philosopher, really likes missing trains. To run after something which is not there is a futile proceeding ; the late arrival for a train is apt not only to look, but, what is worse, to feel both undignified and foolish ; and as there had most certainly been a precedent condition of haste, neither the nerves nor the temper are likely in a normal person to be in the best condition for accepting misfortune gracefully or calmly. And that is why I would like to point out that the missing of a train, which we generally regard as an undiluted, although perhaps slight, misfortune, need not as a rule be regarded as a misfortune at all. True, one's plans are dislocated ; and that is so annoying to some people that if they are going to pay a visit in the country and miss a train they are quite capable of abandoning the whole visit. But it is not such a bad thing to have one's plans dislocated, especially if they are only plans for pleasure. One is obliged to make new arrangements on the spur of the moment, which is always a good thing, awakening alike to the faculties of invention and resource. To the modern mind the chief trouble is that a space of time, probably one or two hours, lies unmapped and unplanned before us ; and there are many to whom such an interval between two prearranged events in their time-table represents sheer vacancy and waste of life. My suggestion is that it should be regarded as pure gain. The train you missed left at three, and there isn't another till five ; you will arrive at your destination in time for dinner instead of tea, and so escape the tiresome, dawdling couple of hours at the beginning of the visit. Here, however, at the other end, are two hours absolutely added to your day, given to you to use and enjoy entirely for your own private advantage. That, I submit, is, in such circumstances, the proper way to look upon the accident of missing a train.

Your first duty is to telegraph to your destination. Failing to arrive by the train one has mentioned is so commonly caused by the accidental missing of it that people should by this time have learned what to do when guests fail to turn up at the station ; but in fact they hardly ever do. The car goes to meet you at the other end ; and when you fail to appear, instead of finding out when the next train is, and putting up near by and returning to meet it, the chauffeur generally returns to head-quarters and reports your non-arrival. It is then just too late, or the man is too busy, for the car to be sent back to meet the second train, and you are thrown upon the resources of the local livery stable. It is a curious fact that the number of trains running to country places is so cunningly devised in proportion to the length of the journey and to the distance from the station of your friend's residence, that a telegram despatched immediately after the train's departure just fails to arrive in time to prevent a horse-drawn vehicle setting forth to meet you. Motor-cars, it is true, have considerably mitigated this aspect of the misadventure ; but even motors have a way of starting unnecessarily early, either to collect parcels in the town or to take some departing person to another train. Anyhow, most railway time-tables were designed before the days of almost universal motor-cars, and the railway companies could not be expected to foresee their advent.

Nevertheless, you send the telegram and discharge your conscience. Having then disposed of your luggage and opened a credit account with the porter who performed prodigies of unavailing speed in trundling it to the closed gates, you set forth from the station a really free man or woman for the next couple of hours. No one except a real enthusiast about railways would think of remaining in a station, for that way lies depression, weariness, and probably indigestion. No, you go forth into the town and for once look about you. I can assure you that the environment even of Liverpool Street or Waterloo may provide you in such circumstances with entertainment at least as engaging as that of Brighton or Scarborough. Usually one only sees such neighbourhoods when beginning or finishing a journey, and has no time to wander about and study them ; yet there are all kinds of interesting and unaccustomed sights there, and you have within yourself the pleasant and unwonted sensation of being in a place not because you are passing through it, but for the simple reason that you choose to be there. There are, it is true, other methods of employing this holiday interval. If you are enterprising enough, and have a sure enough hold on the time-table, you may take a journey by a slow train along your

line to some intermediate station at which the
later train will also stop, and, alighting there,
explore a new town and a new world. It is an
adventurous thing to do, and may turn out well ;
you may make the discovery of your life in Chip-
pendale or Jacobean oak. But you must be prepared
also for its turning out unfortunately. The
railway stations of small provincial towns have a
way of being very remote from what is really the
centre of the town—the church or the High Street,
or the river, or whatever it is you want to see.
A long and depressing road leads from the railway
station into an apparent labyrinth of sordid and
equally depressing streets. You have an instinctive
fear of cutting yourself off by too great a distance
from the station itself. Mistrust of the time-
table seizes you ; for while the missing of one train
may be turned to advantage, to miss two in succes-
sion indicates a certain unfitness for prolonged
sojourn in this vale of tears. Also it may come
on to drizzle, and it may be early closing day in
the wayside town, and in that case the necessity
of spending an hour without an umbrella in a wet
and unknown country town where all the shops
are closed puts you in a worse case than if you had
remained under the steamy and resounding vault
of the original railway-station.

There are many ways, of course, in which the
philosophy outlined in this article may be applied.
If there is a stage on a journey which you have
wished but failed to reach, you derive advantage
from better quarters for the night and an early
start in the morning. If there is a horse or a picture

which you had set your heart on possessing but
which another has secured before you, well, you
may regard yourself as being so many pounds in
pocket, as having a sum to spend or give away
which you would not otherwise have possessed.
If there is an appointment which you hoped and
failed to get you may console yourself by reflecting
that those who had the appointment to give were
obviously not intelligent people, and would not
have been satisfactory to work with. And if there
is a woman you had set your heart on marrying,
and she either could not or would not—well,
perhaps your moment was ill-timed and you missed
the departure of that particular train for
happiness. In that case also I would recommend
not hanging about the station. Take a walk and see
the sights, and come back again in good time ;
perhaps she will have changed her mind and you
may catch the train at last. In the final resort it
is worth remembering that there are other trains,
other stations, and other destinations ; although
this is a somewhat desperate remedy, and is not to
be regarded as bearing on the proper and philo·
sophical method of missing trains.

Sunday Afternoon in England

IT is different from any other afternoon; it has a different melancholy; as different from the dire and squalid gloom of Saturday afternoon as Sunday, which I always think of as showing a glossy black amid the spectroscope of the days, is different from the pale yellow ochre of Saturday. The sense of Sunday will be one of the last things to die in a race that has sat under the shade of Puritanism, and even those people who have never observed the rites of any religion are subject to strange recurring qualms every seventh day, and will be pricked by the desire to do something on that day which is different from their ordinary occupations. It needs no bell or calendar to tell the Anglo-Saxon that it is Sunday; and even if he has forgotten it for the first few hours of the day, it will find him out towards three o'clock in the afternoon. On ships far out at sea, on the burning sands of the desert, on the wide African veldt, in trains storming across the continents, men are every week suddenly remembering that it is Sunday afternoon. I do not know how it may be with others, but with me the sensation is a depressing one. In fact the whole week-end is a very dangerous time. Things which would be grasshoppers on Monday or Wednesday become

156

burdens on Saturday or Sunday. The attack sets
in with acute symptoms early on Saturday afternoon,
when in certain quarters of any town there is a
change in the note of the traffic, a kind of empty
resonance in which the dreadful clangour of the
barrel-organ echoes unchecked. You remember
that it is Saturday afternoon, and therefore a rest
for hundreds of thousands of toiling people, and
you ought to be happy at the thought; but
somehow the thought does not make you happy.
Then is the time that I am first threatened with
panic. What am I doing this afternoon and this
evening, and to-morrow afternoon and to-morrow
evening? A chasm separates me from Monday,
when the wheel of life will begin to turn again;
and if no one has thrown a bridge for me across
it I am certain to be engulfed.

That there is something universal in these
symptoms is shown by the pains people have taken
to relieve them; even for people who do not go to
church there remains the instinct to do something
regularly on Sundays. Hence the Sunday concert,
which for so many people fills the unconfessed but
none the less uncomfortable gap left by a cessation
of public devotional ceremonies. The audiences
at the Queen's Hall and the Albert Hall on
Sunday afternoons are not audiences so much
as congregations. They have the demeanour of
congregations, and they are congregations of a
different religious persuasion. Queen's Hall is
inclined to be High Church; the Albert Hall is
undoubtedly Low Church; indeed the appearance
of the pavement outside after the concert is over,

black with a multitude of respectable people who have finished digesting a heavy dinner and are going home to eat a heavy tea, is like the outside of some vast temple of dissent. But there the analogy ends ; the music inside is happily free from any taint of the atmosphere which it is meant to relieve ; and for thousands of people in London there is at least one hour in which Sunday afternoon is robbed of its terrors.

Yet even here one is in continual danger of the black dog. The mere fact that one so often sits in a certain place on Sunday afternoon and hears certain music becomes dangerous for the music. What if one were to associate it definitely with Sunday afternoons ? Its charm and beauty would be gone ; it would merely call up in one's mind visions of the Albert Memorial or Langham Place, the " morning " coats that still seem to linger in the fashions of the Albert Hall congregations, and the unbridged gulf between now and Monday morning. But happily the music resists these dread influences, partly because at both concerts it is so extremely well chosen. I do not know whether they are aware of it, but the compilers of these programmes have an infinitely more difficult task than they have when they make programmes for any other concerts. Are they aware of what they have to fight against ? Does Sir Henry Wood ever say to himself, " This will do for Wednesday evening, but it will never do for Sunday afternoon ? " Consciously or unconsciously, I think he must ; because although his programmes have nearly always the spirit of afternoon, they never have the spirit of Sunday afternoon.

And what is this spirit? In my case, I am pretty sure that one reason for its depressing influence is that my childish memories of Sunday afternoon are chiefly memories of things forbidden. In the country especially, by the sea, my childish impression was generally that Sunday afternoon was a time terribly wasted. It seems always, moreover, to have been absurdly fine; the rain might pour or a gale blow on Saturday night or Monday morning, but the Sundays of my childhood seem always to have been of a superlative beauty, steeped in sunshine and stillness—days perfectly adapted for doing all the pleasant things forbidden on Sundays. I remember coming out of church and finding the tide brimming up to an unwonted height, the sea like glass, and the stones of the shore visible through the green water to a depth of several feet; the boats dreaming uselessly at their moorings, and all the little creeks and coves among the rocks, navigable only at high water of Spring tides, perforce unvisited by my exploring keel. To Sunday afternoon also seems to belong that memory of the great heat stored up in the woodwork of a boat lying on the beach, and of the unwonted feeling of treading on the shifting pebbles on the beach in patent-leather Sunday shoes. The feeling, moreover, that a wet rope was a thing that might damage or soil one's clothes was a feeling entirely associated with Sunday. My further grudge against these summer Sundays of long ago is that on those days I was a child ravished from my sea pursuits and forced to inland occupations; obliged to contemplate the flowers in walled gardens, and take walks over rolling turf and amid groves of trees from which not even a view of the sea could be obtained. Church I accepted as inevitable and (granted the necessity of going there at all) not without interests of its own; but the waste of the sunshine and the high tide out of doors was a thing that seemed unreasonable and unjustifiable. It is curious how false one's memory may be: for as in my recollection the Sundays were always fine, so was the tide always brim-high about one o'clock—a thing impossible in nature. And I remember no Sunday afternoon which had that empty feeling, caused by the tide being low and the shore ugly with misshapen and unfamiliar seaweeds, that made even the sea distasteful during week-day hours.

But I am grateful for the rule which obliged me to do different things on Sundays from what I did on other days. I cannot help thinking that the modern fashion of allowing children to do only what they like is a bad one; for there are many things which children are glad in after years to have done, which they would never do of their own choice and initiative. Among these, perhaps, the restrictions of Sunday and the apparent waste of its golden afternoons may be counted. Something still and shining hovers on the horizon of memory where they lie; something that punctuated and divided life, solemnly perhaps, but simply and not unhappily. I was reminded of it when I saw in a visitor's book in a little inn in Cornwall the verses in which Professor Blackie had sung the praises of Mary Munday's hospitality,

enjoyed by him in that little cottage inn that
lies between Mullion Church and the sea ; a place
half hidden in the angle of the road, where the
church dreams in a peace as of the eternal
Sabbath, and no rumour or drift of spray from the
shouting sea ever reaches the sheltered graveyard.

> And I advise you all to hold
> By the well-tried things that are good and old,
>   Like this old house of Munday ;
> The old church and the old inn,
> And the old way to depart from sin
>   By going to church on Sunday.

Certainly the Carlton and the Albert Hall are
poor substitutes.

A Morning Adventure

I AM not what is called an early riser. On the other hand, I sit up late at night. It seems to me just as human and meritorious a proceeding, although the copy-books give one no credit for it. It has always been a custom to sneer at the man who lies abed while the rest of the world is up and doing; but the merits of the man who remains up and doing while the rest of the world is snoring under blankets have never been sufficiently recognised. Such is the force of inherited prejudice, however, that I feel no pride in my nightly feat of sitting up reading or talking till the small hours, whereas, if by any chance I do get up fairly early in the morning, I am filled with an unwonted sense of virtue and heroism, and behave as if I accepted all the conventional superstitions—that a man who rises early has a sense of buoyancy and clarity of mind, and inspires in these early hours a store of energy lasting throughout a long day. The truth with me is exactly the contrary. If I sit up till two in the morning and rise at nine, I feel fit and well and have as much appetite for work as it is possible for me to have, and a zest for any kind of amusement that the day may bring which is, I am glad to say, unfailing. If, on the contrary, I go to bed at half-past ten and get up at six I spend the night in stark wakefulness, and go out into the world with a sense of heroism, it is true, but also with a slight sense of dissipation. I have a faint burning sensation in the eyes, feel strangely languid and drowsy, am incommoded by the sensation that I have swallowed and am carrying about with me a smouldering coal, have no appetite whatever for breakfast, and probably doze off into an uneasy slumber about 11 A.M. Mere early rising—getting up before other people, that is to say—seems to me an overrated virtue, chiefly esteemed as a means of getting the better of other people. We all know the proverbial breakfast of the early bird. Well, I do not want the fattest worm; I am more than content that someone else should have it; and a little bit of a quite lean one will do for me, provided that I am let alone to choose for myself what I think desirable, and to fix the standard by which I shall measure my own wisdom or folly.

All the same, as I say, I got up this morning and went out to taste the first breath of summer in London streets that were strangely unfamiliar. All the houses in my neighbourhood were shut and shuttered as in the middle of August; the streets were almost empty except for a few pedestrians of an unfamiliar kind. A group of house-breakers were assembling to begin their dusty job of destruction; a chimney-sweep was wheeling a little hand-cart full of brushes and soot, with the legend " Established 1851 " painted on it; and this furnished me with some reflections on the nature of pride, and on how, even in being a chimney-

sweep for threescore years and ten, there may be
something more than labour and sorrow. Cats
sat unashamed in the middle of roadways which
at other hours are filled with the brimming tide of
wheeled traffic, and there were long unwonted
vistas, such as the lion on Dickens' and Jones' shop
in Regent Street seen in a perspective from
Park Lane, a suggestion of blue hills filling
the opening of Orchard Street, and the spire of
Harrow Church standing apparently at the end of
Park Street. There were no taxis nor motor-
omnibuses running, but I found a hansom which
took me at an agreeable trot along the empty
streets. And the first discovery that I made was
that London, at any rate in the West End, goes
back to her more innocent ways in these early
morning hours. Motor-cars are almost entirely
absent, hansom-cab drivers, milkmen, dustmen,
and costermongers alone occupying the thoroughfares, and there is peace and silence, and taste of
the old thrill of a more sober, spacious, and
dignified London.

My destination was Covent Garden, for I had
never seen Covent Garden in the early morning;
that being one of the many exciting and agreeable
things which all Londoners are supposed to have
done, and many pretend to have done, but few in
fact have done. All the rest of the West End was
deserted, but in the neighbourhood of Garrick
Street my hansom was blocked by a line of carts
bearing fruit and flowers and vegetables. Here
I met a friend by appointment, and together we
strolled for a little round a network of streets all

of which were entirely filled with carriers' horse-drawn carts. Whoever else was asleep, there was plenty of life going on here, and as yet we were only on the outskirts. How the traffic changes from hour to hour in these narrow London thoroughfares! One hour of the day they will be traversed by heavy motor-vans, and those huge waggons that the railway companies scatter from their stations; at another hour there will be nothing but lines of carriages and motors and taxicabs, with shining lamps and varnish, and throngs of liveried servants; but now there was nothing but the smell of flowers and fruit, and brilliant splashes of colour, and horses tossing their nosebags, and all the ancient business of collecting and distributing the fruits of the earth. One was continually being jostled by people bearing pine boxes which might contain any edible vegetable thing from onions to strawberries, from mushrooms to asparagus; the wilderness had blossomed like the rose, and the morning air smelled like a garden. All the porters and burden bearers were engaged on the same business, and knew and greeted each other; but we felt like idlers and strangers who had strayed into a foreign city where we did not know the language. As we drew nearer to the centre of this great commotion of flowers and fruit the throng became denser, and the menace of wooden boxes swiftly borne on broad shoulders became greater. I have said that the scene was curiously foreign; and so it was, but only perhaps because a Londoner is more familiar with such scenes in foreign places than in his own town. There were

certainly two particularly English characteristics
in the occasion. One was its silence. There was
practically no shouting, and not much conversation,
and as the commodities were all being carried
by hand from the market to the waiting carts in
the adjacent streets there was little sound of traffic
other than of feet on the pavement. In any
foreign town there would have been yelling and
gesticulating, a carnival of sound as well as of
movement. Even in Ireland or in Scotland what
I remember of such morning scenes is that they
are accompanied by loud shouting. But here the
swift streams of movement ran quietly, and those
who greeted each other did not need to raise their
voices. And the other notable thing was the
extraordinary order and efficiency with which the
whole business of transportation was carried out.
Everything, even the purchase, seemed to have
been settled long ago. It was as if people were
carrying out, not a commercial transaction of the
moment, but a law of nature as old as mankind.
The organisation was perfect ; it was not an
artificial or a disciplined organisation, but a natural
organisation. In France or Germany or Belgium,
for example, there would have been policemen
and officials at every corner ; queues would have
been formed, and the whole business carried on
under the iron hand of authority. But here the
order was natural and spontaneous, like that of
people long used to seemly and efficient ways. Out
of this great cornucopia a delicious plenty of colour
and light was flowing in immense volume, and in
every direction, but, as I said, the organisation was

spontaneous; the flood had not to be kept in by dykes and groins and embankments; it ran in natural channels that Time and itself had worn, and ran without inconvenience or risk or confusion.

And now I am nearly falling asleep, having done little justice to my theme. For that you must blame this indulgence in the virtue of early rising, and the fact that when I should have been quietly asleep in my bed I was idling and dissipating among the flowers. The next time I go to Covent Garden I shall stay up all night; I shall then merely go to bed a little later than usual, and rise a little later— a much more orderly proceeding.

Christmas Presents

CHRISTMAS shopping is an invention of the devil whereby people are induced to purchase things that are of no value, and give them to other people who do not want them. It has also the effect, during any of the four weeks preceding Christmas, of turning the purchase of any simple article in a shop into an adventure that is something between a battle and a nightmare. For the shopkeeper at this season thinks it necessary to put into the background the more or less useful things which it is his habit to sell, and to import into his shop a quantity of flimsy rubbish known as " The Season's Goods," " Suitable Gifts for Xmas," " Useful Presents," and " Artistic Gifts." Not one in a hundred of these articles is either useful, artistic, or seasonable. Most of them are substantive lies, made to look passably like the thing which they imitate for about a week. After that, fortunately, they begin to disintegrate ; for if Christmas gifts were not of a perishable nature the world would soon be piled so high with rubbish and shams that no true or genuine thing could exist on it. Here and there this transitory nature of the Christmas gift causes distress, as when the deluded recipient finds the gorgeous present coming to pieces in his hands at the first attempt to put it to genuine use ; but it is an apparent rather than a real affliction. Here and there, in the darker corners of any house you may come upon the Christmas present of a year or two ago in a state of arrested decay ; and a grisly relic it is. Parts of it resemble plush, and other parts tarnished gold or silver, other parts are almost unrecognisable ; but careful examination will probably reveal it as a representation of a pig stooping over a trough, and bearing a label with the legend " For what we are about to receive." What was its purpose ? Was it a pen-wiper, or a receptacle for pins, or —for we must not flinch in our research—was it possibly intended to contain salt upon the table, or was it an ash-tray ? Even echo does not answer.

I have before me several advertisements on a page of a daily newspaper, all purporting to give me real assistance in the choice of Christmas presents. Here is a list from one of them, headed " Suitable Xmas Gifts " : carpets and rugs, fancy linens, down quilts, children's chairs, antiques, gramophones, Oriental ware, clocks and bronzes, electric lamps, fancy goods. Of course, I am greatly helped by this. I have now merely to decide for myself whether I shall give my friend some fancy linen, a child's chair, a carpet, or an electric lamp. What I will not buy in any circumstances is fancy goods. I do not know exactly what they are, but I know them to be the abomination of desolation ; and I believe them to be the shopkeepers' name for the things which he cannot even pretend are of any use, and which do not even look like anything

else on earth. Fancy Goods! In what desolate
fancy are they conceived; to what degraded fancy
do they appeal? And here is a nasty thing:
"Caned fire-screen. In birch, stained walnut,
reproduced from quaint old model." It is not itself
quaint, or old, or walnut, you see; and it is of
course flimsy and perishable; one of those turned
knobs will almost instantly disappear, and it will
ultimately be found kicking about in some dark
corner, and will trip up some unoffending housemaid
whose indigent employer has failed to keep up her
Insurance book, and will consequently be heavily
fined and have to maintain her for a long time in
hospital, so that he will be ultimately ruined and his
children go begging in the streets.

And here is another list of suggestions also called
"Useful Presents": attaché-cases, book-carriers,
hand-bags, writing-cases, card-tables, "library re-
quisities of every description." These, if you are
unlucky enough to receive them all, may be put
to a variety of uses. You may either put the writing-
case in the book-carrier, and carry it, or you
may put the hand-bag into the attaché-case and
pretend that you are an Attaché, or you may fold
up the book-carrier tightly, put in the hand-bag,
and put both in the writing-case into the attaché-
case and lay it on the card-table. As for the library
requisites, you had better leave them alone. One
of the outrages I have suffered was in the re-
ception of a Christmas gift in the form of a thing
which I imagine to have been a library requisite.
It was a mauve box which purported to be of leather,
but in fact was fabricated in some preparation of

dyed paper. It had an imitation gold clasp which broke off as I opened it. My deepest misgivings were fulfilled. It contained three compartments, one of them filled with many-coloured balls resembling small marbles, which on investigation proved to be an impure kind of sealing-wax. Another compartment contained an ugly little instrument of imitation silver, in which the balls were supposed to be melted; another a seal, engraved with the initial letter of my name and fitted with a handle made of some explosive substance, pretending to be a precious stone. It was the cause of the only moment of doubt and disappointment I ever knew with regard to my secretary; for when I asked her to take it away and have it destroyed, she said she would like to keep it.

But the crowning terror of Christmas-time is the calendar. Here it is, of course, on the page in front of me: " Beautiful Art Calendars." You know them. There is hardly any kind of shop which does not at this time include in its wares a collection of calendars; and there is no kind of ugly or false thing which cannot be adapted to the purposes of a calendar. The most familiar form, and not the least offensive, is a collection of large sheets of stiff paper held together by a coloured ribbon, by which they are to be suspended on the wall. A large legend in some kind of base lettering will probably announced that it is " To give you greeting." Underneath will be the word " January," with a photogravure picture of an old woman collecting sticks in the neighbourhood of a church, with either a line of verse descriptive of the state of the weather, or a sentence from some prose work expressive of stalwart purpose in life. And somewhere in the corner there will be a faint little table of the days of the month. What may be on the other sheets hardly matters, for even in the most pious home the calendar is abandoned long before the middle of the year has gone. Through January it hangs crookedly from a gas bracket ; and through February also the January legend and picture are still exposed ; because the mechanical problem of turning the front page over the blue ribbon is regarded as insoluble, and to tear it off would be to spoil the calendar. Late in February, having become darker round the edges and curling hideously, and having collected a deposit of dust, it is removed to the kitchen, where the February page is exposed, revealing a woodland scene through which a little girl in a red cap is wending her solitary way carrying a basket. And having thus existed throughout March, curled by the kitchen heat almost into the form of a cylinder, it is suddenly removed on a cleaning day, is never replaced, and disappears thenceforth from the sight of man. But that is only one of the simplest forms of the Christmas calendar. Sometimes it takes the form of a little book the size of a postage stamp " for the waistcoat pocket," which will subsequently be found in the kind of drawer in which servants keep wire and corks and dusters and string and brushes. Or it may take the form of a dog, or a church tower, or a stuffed plush bear with eyes made of beads, or a very expensive leather case, or a pipe, or a little boat with sails, or a framed

picture with the calendar inserted in the frame—
of anything at all, in fact.

This is not a nice spirit in which to write of
Christmas presents ; but after all it is only the
shopman's idea of Christmas to which I take exception. I object to its seizure and exploitation
as a great commercial event. There is no joy
in that or any real good for anybody. It is not
a good thing to give employment to people in
making rubbish, and it is as a lover of this season
that I am grieved to see it made a festival of ugliness
and imposture. A world that sits surrounded by a
collection of sham articles—sham in substance,
base in design, false in sentiment, and vain in
purpose, is putting too much on the bells when it
asks them to " ring out the false, ring in the true."

A Dog

VERY trivial beginnings come to great
ends. Our beginning, twelve years ago,
was in a shop in Great Portland Street,
where I saw a small fox-terrier puppy
whining in a cage, and suddenly realised that for the
sum of thirty shillings I could take him out of it. I
paid, and took him. He disgraced me on the way
home, and exposed me to indignant contumely. If I
stopped to speak to him he cowered on his belly and
whined ; when I tried to lead him on the leash
he assumed the attitude of a tortoise, and had
to be dragged along in such a way that humane
people looked askance at me, saying, " There is a
monster : even his dog knows his black heart,
and will not follow him." I found that he suffered
from both rickets and cataract. The second
complaint was cured by a vet. ; the first gradually
yielded to good food and fresh air, and to an apple
suspended from a piece of string under the
bough of an apple-tree, with which he was never
tired of playing. And gradually, too, he began
to dare to walk erect upon his legs, and not to
collapse if he were spoken to ; whatever memories
of human cruelty were in his heart gradually
faded from it, and gave place to a kind of surprised
conviction that not everybody wished to hurt

him. But all the inconvenient things that a young dog can do, he did. The art of being sick was carried by him to amazing lengths; he had stronger appetites, and a weaker stomach, than any dog I ever knew, and the moments which he chose for his demonstrations were wonderful in their combination of unexpectedness, inconvenience, and humiliation for his owner. But his own humility was such that he invariably apologised for drawing attention to himself. The latter half of his body was entirely devoted to the demonstration of this humility. If he stood barking (for he soon learned to bark) with his forepaws planted firmly, his squirming rearpart would apologise for barking. When he ate, his tail wagged apology. When, an hour afterwards, he was sick, the tail vibrated like that of a rattlesnake. If he was drinking, and I happened to cough or make any sound, he would leave his bowl with dripping jaws, quivering apology for having presumed to satisfy his thirst. And there were other necessary and natural functions which he could in nowise be brought to perform except by a studied aversion of gaze on the part of his master, who, standing in the garden on a wet night, had to pretend to be studying the heavens. Every attempt to notice him evoked a silent paraphrase of the reply of Uriah Heep: "Thank you, sir; we know our station, and are thankful in it."

But that phase passed. Time taught him that he was indeed of some consequence in this world, and that he might retain his food without danger of appearing to be unduly presumptuous. And with this knowledge dawned an affection, a capacity for love and devotion, that proved to be the great theme and tragedy of his life. He had his doggy ways and appetites, but they were ever subordinate to the following of his human star—or stars; for happily there were both sun and stars in his heaven, and all shone benignantly upon him. It was his lot to spend many changeful and wandering years with me, now in this place, now in that: in railway trains, in boats, by strange firesides, in field and street, on roads and commons. He witnessed the morning of the motor movement, and travelled many a thousand miles tucked under my left arm while I steered, knowing well that independent movement was not allowed, and staring always, with the true motoring habit, out on the strip of road that flowed and wriggled before us, snuffing anxiously the while, and taking heaven knows what complicated bearings, and registering endless smells and views, lest haply it should be required of him to retrace the long way alone. And after motoring days were over it was long before he broke himself off the habit of leaping into any motor-car he saw standing still; for what he had early learned about motor-cars was that there was only one place to be, and that was inside them. Most of us know it now, but he knew it from the first.

One of his great trials was the sea, for it happened that at one time I was much upon the sea, and it was a case of choosing whether to come and suffer, or to be left at home in stomachic security. He always chose the nobler part. When the dinghy

came alongside the slip, his lips would draw away
from his set teeth in disgusted anticipation, but he
would leap in; when it drew alongside the boat
I sailed in he would be the first on board, and
hastily, like a model passenger retire to the depths,
out of the way of hurrying feet and slatting ropes.
Thereafter, when the floor on which he lay became
unstable, he would uneasily shift his position,
looking at me with reproachful eyes; and presently,
after moving rapidly over the floor boards with his
back humped like a camel's, would take his stand
swayingly in a public position, and deliver himself
over to the crisis in a way that indicated his intention
of doing full justice to it. The rest would be an
uneasy, dreaming doze, with a final emergence on
deck and snuffing of the land as we approached,
and whining, barking, and tail-wagging threats
to throw himself into the water and swim to the
converging shore.

Those were days of youth and adventure; later
days brought him, as they should, a sense of ease
and security and dignity, in a world of love tempered
by hunger. For he had his besetting weakness—
what dog worth the name has not? His was ashpits.
He would as soon have thought of drowning himself
as of stealing at home; but oh, the delicious combination of blood and sawdust at the door of a
butcher's shop, and the grisly treasures to be
snatched there; and oh, the fearful joys of heaps
that appeared to be nothing but ashes and egg-shells,
but that, in fact, like life itself, contained pearls of
price for those who could diligently seek! They
were well worth the conscience-stricken return

home, and almost worth the days of abstinence that followed. . It is the time he spends in eating that a dog values—not the quantity of nourishment he gets. He was dieted like a Marienbad patient, and his dinner consisted of carefully selected food of the finest quality ; but what was that compared with the long, barren chewing at a fowl's leg, or the guilty gulping of some unidentified organic substance that could be measured, not in inches, but in feet ? His earthly friends were supreme with him, but his god was his belly, and it was a god that instantly responded to any sacrifice offered to it. Latterly it seldom rejected any. His figure, since a fat fox-terrier is a misery to himself and his friends, was a matter of constant watchful consideration and discussion. Members of his family who had been absent from him for a time would be eagerly asked if he looked any thinner, and it was considered tactless to say he did not. If he escaped for half an hour he would come back distinctly fatter, and be overcome by a strange and far from silent sleep. If it was thought that he had come down a little too fine, it could be put right in one meal ; but if he had to be reduced, it was a matter of anxious weeks spent on a task which might be frustated by one moment's lack of vigilance. Yet no mess of food ever existed that he would not leave, and leave gladly, at the sound of a voice that he loved. If it is chiefly on his material weakness that I have dwelt, it is because his strength was spiritual and unspeakable ; because the affections of his heart, that were his true life, cannot be measured or described to those to whom he was not dear.

And suddenly he died, falling like a shock of corn when it is ripe and perfect ; without pain, without struggle, with the hands about him that had meant human care and protection and love. It is only to a friendly audience that one could speak of him, and I like to think of my readers as not unfriendly to anything that is humanly concerning to any of us. I can raise no stone to him ; but I may be forgiven for making this little funeral celebration. He was a part of life as I know it. And as we do not live or grow save gradually, so we die, not suddenly, but by degrees ; every parting is a little death. There are griefs that it is weak to indulge, idle to dwell upon, useless to communicate ; one can only try to change them into something else.

. . . Where is he to-night ? Where shall I look for him ? Not in the empty basket ; not in his eternal bed under the orchard grass. Not here or there, I swear, but everywhere in the universe where there is love, and the happiness that love brings, shall that little spirit inhabit, as fresh and fragrant as the blossom of the apple-trees under which he rests.

Printed in Great Britain at
The Mayflower Press, Plymouth.
William Brendon & Son, **Ltd.**

8|